where the heart is

Books by Florence Roe Wiggins

Strawberry Point
Strawberry Point Kitchens
Love's Gift
Where The Heart Is

where the heart is

Florence Roe
Wiggins

Christian Herald Books
40 Overlook Drive, Chappaqua, New York 10514

Grateful acknowledgement is made to the following:

Part of the chapter "The Porcelain Cup of Friendship" was first
published in *Daily Meditation* in November 1961. (Reprinted by
permission of *Daily Meditation* © 1961 All rights reserved.)

Part of the chapter "Wise Words from a Great Woman" first appeared as
an essay entitled "Talent Is a Responsibility" in *Church Musician* in June
1973. (Reprinted by permission of *Church Musician* © 1973. The
Sunday School Board of the Southern Baptist Convention. All rights
reserved.)

Portions of three essays and one poem appeared first in *The Christian
Science Monitor* as "Satisfaction of a Career in Homemaking" (March 12,
1968), "A Flower for Dame Myra (March 2, 1965), "Women's Lib
Includes Losses" (September 29, 1972), and "The Path of Light" (January
22, 1966). Reprinted by permission from *The Christian Science Monitor*.
Copyrights 1968, 1965, 1972, and 1966 by The Christian Science
Publishing Society. All rights reserved.

For Reynold

CONTENTS

Preface viii
A Night in Dallas 1
A Career Woman Looks at Homemaking 8
Career and the Baby 19
A Modern Miracle 26
The Porcelain Cup of Friendship 34
The Kitchen: Home's Heart 42
Food for the Spirit 48
A Penny—Saved and Spent 55
Gather 'Round to Sing a Song 60
Train Up a Child 69
The New Woman 78
Weathering Storms 88
Wise Words from a Great Woman 111
The Path of Light Leads Home 126

PREFACE

NOT LONG AGO a newspaper with a national and international readership published two articles of opposing convictions on the subject of the woman in the home. One of those articles was mine and is included in this book in the chapter, "The New Woman." The reaction to those articles was strong and varied, and letters reached the editorial office from all parts of the United States as well as from England, Germany and India. They later were published as an entire page in the newspaper.

From these letters I learned a great deal. Specifically, I found out that women from all parts of the world are profoundly troubled by the trend of the times, the trend away from the home; they are troubled by the universally accepted belief that the home has failed. Most of the women who wrote these letters are in complete disagreement with the cynical outlook upon home and family relationships, believing not that the home has failed people but perhaps people are failing the home.

One letter in particular gave me considerable insight into the subject. Written by a woman who lives in St. Louis, it said in part: "Mrs. Wiggins is a happy example of a liberated woman. Her attitude hints that her added training enhanced her ability as a homemaker for she is deeply satisfied with what she has done. This kind of liberation doesn't rob the home—it enhances it." Until I read that letter I never had thought of myself as a "liberated" woman; neither had I thought of myself as an enslaved one. Soap boxes and crusades are not for me, nor is the championing of causes. But I must admit that using my talents to enhance my home has proved to be deeply satisfying.

In my experience I have found that it is not necessarily talent or a career that is responsible for wrecking a home. I strongly believe that each woman needs all her abilities to build a warm and and satisfying home. In this book I have simply gathered together personal experiences in the establishment of *one* happy home, hoping they may be helpful to others who are faced with similar challenges and who are seeking "this kind of liberation."

Florence Roe Wiggins

MY HOME

I thought
to build my home
upon a hill, with stepping
stones that gaily tripped up to
my door.

But now
I know that home
is not a place, but peace
within the heart, its path well paved
with love.

from the book
Love's Gift

where
the
heart
is

A NIGHT IN DALLAS

AS WE DROVE into Dallas that cold night, gusts of rain beat against the car's windshield and street lights were a dim, yellow blur. The atmosphere inside the car was equally cold. My husband was as depressed as I was. Ordinarily on a long, tiresome trip, Reynold or I would start singing and we would quickly sing our way out of boredom. But that night, as we rode along in complete silence, I did not even take refuge in dreams about the future, the time when we would once again live what I fondly thought of as a "normal" life.

For over three years we had been living out of a suitcase—in hotels—even when we were "off the road." It was war-time. To find an apartment in San Francisco where we were stationed part of the time was an impossibility. We had sold our pretty home in the Southland; our precious family treasures were in storage. The day when we could again enjoy a home was dim and remote, receding as the light of the passing cars.

We had been travelling by car that spring. My husband, a theatrical booking agent, had many calls to make in college towns and on out-of-the-way college campuses, extremely difficult to reach by plane or train. Now, we were on our way back to California, and San Francisco seemed a long, long way from Dallas.

The motel that night was as cheerless as the streets. The radio was dead and the dim light from the single ceiling bulb was too poor for reading. Both Reynold and I were sobered by the dismal room and the constant drip, drip of the soggy night. Conversation languished until suddenly my husband cleared his throat and began to speak as though he were reciting a well-rehearsed speech.

"I've been doing a lot of serious thinking on this trip," he said, "and I realize this life on the road is much too hard on you. I have decided that when we reach Los Angeles I am going to resign from this job and find work there that will allow us to have a real home again."

For many months I had longed to hear those words. I had never adjusted to the make-believe world of the theatre and I was not impressed by the glamorous life behind the footlights. However, now that Reynold actually spoke those words I felt none of the elation I had expected to feel. Suddenly, I sensed—no, I knew what this decision had cost my husband. This work he loved had been interrupted by World War I, by six long years of ill health, and by the equally long depression of the thirties. I remembered how happy he had been the day a former employer had called him and offered to recommend him for this work. He loved the exciting new contacts, the constantly changing scenes, associating with talent and the promotion of stimulating and worthwhile entertainment. And now he was offering to give up all this to please me.

"Play it light," I thought to myself and I laughed as I said, "Cheer up. The weather is getting you down. Tomorrow the sun will shine, and you'll have a good day in Dallas."

I lay awake a long time that night. In that moment of crisis it did not occur to either one of us that I should stay in the Southland while Reynold was travelling. That would be a compromise—and we had never needed to have recourse to compromises. We had always worked out our problems together, and he had made me feel that it was important that I travel with him. Now, however, I realized if I rejected his sacrifice and determined to continue travelling with him, I would have to change my attitude toward this kind of life. If this life was good for my husband, it *must* be good for me, too. I could not go on indefinitely pretending something I did not feel. Self-pity would be sure to surface when I least wanted it to. Somehow, someway, I reasoned, there must be a right solution—a right answer for me, too.

And then I thought of my sampler. It was a bit of linen that I had been painstakingly embroidering during the many weeks of travel. I had purchased it in San Francisco the day we left on this trip, hoping it would help me while away the hours when Reynold was attending to business.

"We are travelling," I explained to the clerk who

waited on me. "I want something small and not too complicated—something not too bulky."

"This may appeal to you," she had answered as she unfolded a small square of linen, stamped with a picture of a quaint little house in a tiny, fenced-in garden. Underneath, spelled out in German text, were the words, "Home Is Where The Heart Is."

"The design is simple, but worked in cross-stitching, it is effective," the clerk said.

"It doesn't look too difficult," I replied with an amused smile. "Somehow I believe I shall enjoy working it."

All this came back to me in that moment of self-examination. "How could I have so disregarded the sentiment of the little motto," I thought, "when I had spent so many happy hours cross-stitching its message."

"Where is your home, anyway?" I now asked myself, and the answer came quickly. "Where it has always been. Not on a hilltop, not by the sea, not even in the Southland."

My home would always be where my heart was. And that meant at my husband's side, wherever his travels took him. In the half light I looked at Reynold asleep. I saw the young man I first loved, then the wounded war veteran, now the man who fully enjoyed his career. He was offering to give up the life he loved to please me. Instantly, I knew I could never accept such a sacrifice from my husband. At that moment what was best for him became best for me too. With that decision, there came to me a deep sense of well-being and personal happiness. I was content.

From that day on I carried my home with me. Every hotel or motel room became a challenge. First I unpacked suitcases and put away all signs of travel. I found that a few personal possessions can transform a room from being cold, ordinary and impersonal to a home, warm and loved. A few favorite books, a leather-framed photograph of our daughter "in college," a plate for fruit or candy, a vase for a flower or two, magazines on a table, a knitting bag on the back of a chair—and we are at home.

And when my husband returned from business, it was more than a homey room he wanted to see. I made sure I was an interesting person and I made it my business to become well informed about each city or town we visited. I kept a chronicle and recorded any unusual experiences or important information about each place. Very often, in later years, this diary of events proved of great value. My memories are clear and immediate, not to mention their worth as sources for my writing.

Strangely enough, or perhaps, it was not so strange after all—for right thinking, I am convinced, does open channels that seem irrevocably closed—on our return to San Francisco we found an apartment waiting for us! We rented it over the telephone. On our way out to view this prize, Reynold warned me, "Now, remember, it's not Nob Hill. It is in the fog district out near the

Park. Probably it will only have windows on the front and the back. And there will be no San Francisco atmosphere, for it is brand new."

"Well, if it is new, at least it will be clean," I said. "And as far as sunshine is concerned we'll make our own if it has a kitchen." (I had shared a kitchen the summer before with three navy wives.)

That day as we stood in the kitchen with its bleak view from the one, tiny window, I was quiet, lost in thought.

"Penny," Reynold said.

"My thoughts aren't that valuable," I said. "I was just thinking how to furnish this windowless dining area of the kitchen. I believe there will be room for your rocker and a shelf of books. Maybe I can turn it into an old-fashioned kitchen with my braided rug. We won't miss a window so much if we hang some pictures, too."

"For better or for worse," Reynold quoted softly. "Mostly worse, I think sometimes. What a lot of kitchens you've made homelike during the past twenty years."

"It has been fun," I said, "a sort of challenge. These twenty years have been the happiest ones of my life." And I meant it.

This little flat with its tiny, wood-burning fireplace, with its five rooms and five windows, became heaven itself to us for several years each time we returned from a trip.

Home may broaden its roof and enlarge its borders but when well fortified, it will hold its own. Oliver Wendell Holmes has defined home in a way that is a help to any family that must lead a nomadic existence. "Where we love is home," he wrote, "home that our feet may leave but not our hearts." And that is precisely the rewarding decision I made on that bleak and rainy night in Dallas, Texas, so many years ago.

A CAREER WOMAN LOOKS AT HOMEMAKING

BUILDING A HAPPY HOME began twenty years before that important night in Dallas. It was during my last year in college that the first stones in the foundation were laid.

February of my senior year brought significant changes in my plans. That school year I had been very busy. To capture two degrees (B.S. and B.M.) in one year with all the recitals and programs involved was in itself a task Hercules might have balked at. But it was all work that I loved. At that time my only thought was directed toward collecting my honorary degrees and preparing for my parents' graduation gift: a summer in California and a trip to Florida with them the following winter.

But after the February Sorority Formal, I began secretly to work toward another achievement. That dance was a memorable evening. As president of my sorority, I and my escort were in the receiving line and led the Grand March. Reynold Wiggins, the young man who worked at the conservatory as secretary, was my date for the evening. We had been good friends for two years but not dating steadily. However, on that evening it was as though I, in my ivory taffeta and lace, and he, in his first tux, were seeing each other for the first time. We were no longer casual friends on an evening date, but suddenly a man and woman with stars in our eyes.

We were double dating that night with the director of the conservatory and a sorority sister of mine. The four of us were the best of friends and on this night we were in an especially happy mood. The men had delayed ordering a taxi until none was available, and they arrived for us in, of all things, a lumbering, antiquated hearse! We were hilarious all the way to the dance but coming home Reynold and I were very quiet, quite oblivious to the conveyance. Risser and Mabel left us at my door and that night I accepted Reynold's fraternity pin.

My sudden engagement made me painfully aware of my need to prepare for the duties of running a home. My mother had the mistaken idea that if I knew nothing about the kitchen, I would never be called upon to do anything there. I was really domestically inclined but our kitchen at home was presided over by a domestic tyrant. Ada was an excellent cook and kept our house immaculate, but she welcomed no interference in her domain. Later there were other "Adas," but very few held open house for me.

One time when I was in High School, I remember that the present Ada complained to Mother that I was insisting on coming into the kitchen to make fudge and it drew flies. Mother, bless her heart, said crisply, "Then we'll have flies." Nevertheless, the ability to make a pan of fudge doesn't prepare a young bride for running a home.

In spite of being completely unprepared for my coming duties, I was confident that, once I knew the routine, I would manage two careers and make a success of both of them. In all fairness to my hard-working parents, I knew I must prove that my expensive education had not been wasted. I really wanted to compose music, and I thought it would fit beautifully into a career of homemaking.

Preparation for running a home, I soon began to realize, was something I could not learn from a book. I did try. I sent for six volumes called *The Library of Cooking and Dressmaking,* which I studied diligently every moment I could spare. But homemaking, I found, consisted of far more than skill in the kitchen or learning how to hold a needle.

I began to examine the homes I admired to see what it was that gave them charm and hominess. My parents' home lacked these qualities, for the efficient Ada, who kept the house painstakingly clean, wasted no loving thought upon it. Mother helped Father in his photograph studio. Her interests were there. This family circumstance did give me a few qualms about trying to combine two careers, but I comforted myself with the thought that music would be so much a part of my home that my two careers would complement each other.

I began to take special note of the beautiful homes in our college town. We music majors were often called upon to furnish the entertainment for large affairs in such homes. I was especially eager to attend such functions now, and to store for my future home original and appealing ideas that came my way. Not that I aspired to own a mansion. My husband-to-be was putting himself through school—working for his meals and serving as secretary of the conservatory for his tuition. I realized, even then, that our new home was going to be built on values, not on things.

One day I was called to furnish the program at a tea in a home near the campus. The grand piano stood near French doors that led into a sun room—a gay room furnished in brightly cushioned wicker furniture. As I started to sing, a little canary in the sun room joined me, warbling a lovely obligato accompaniment. All during the recital he continued to support my songs and never once was his contribution off key, but blended consistently in harmony with my voice. On that day I took some important mental notes. Not about the expensive and beautiful furnishings, but about the delight that a small yellow bird can bring to a home where music is loved.

Today you will find in my home, not far from my piano, a bright yellow canary, by name George the Third, and his sweet obligato accompaniment to my music symbolizes for me the harmony that came into my home with his predecessor many years ago.

There were many residences in that modestly affluent community that expressed excellent taste in furnishings and appointments. My friend Jeanette lived in one such home and I was a frequent visitor there. I began to take special note of the value of flowers in making a home attractive, of the appreciation evident for art and color. Jeanette's older sister taught art appreciation in our college, and I hastened to add that elective course to my already over-full schedule.

Perhaps the home in our college town that influenced my future home the most was that of three of my sorority sisters, Grace, Dora and Margie Sailor. It was a comfortable home, full of love and laughter, where boys and girls from the campus were always welcome. I gained the impression that, to this home, money and the things that money could buy were somehow unimportant. Both parents were interesting people, public spirited, deeply religious, vitally involved in community affairs. The talented mother, although she was a capable homemaker (I remember her cooky jar was never long empty) was, at that time, promoting a literary venture known as the Shakespeare Club. It was an organization that now is an important part of the city's cultural life and was recently lauded in the newspapers for its service to the community, when its new home was dedicated and the memory of its founder, Mrs. Sailor, was honored.

Mr. Sailor was especially interested in the girls' courses of study and took great pleasure in helping them with their homework. I remember the year that Margie and I were studying geology (under a rather dull professor); Mr. Sailor gave up many a Sunday afternoon to join us on rambles over the countryside as we searched for rock specimens.

This home was so much my ideal of what a home should be that I often expressed the hope to Reynold that we could pattern ours after it. In fact, I chose the date of the Sailors' wedding anniversary for our wedding day. "Maybe some of their successful home life will rub off on us," I said to Reynold.

For two years before I married I held a position on the faculty of the small conservatory of music from which I graduated. While I was still in school, the director called on me to help choose the music for the spring pageants. With the director's able assistance, I was soon able to choreograph my own dances. It often seemed that she expected miracles from me. However, I have been grateful many times since then for the rigorous training I received.

The year after graduation I was called back to choreograph the dances and train the dancers for the senior operetta. The operetta was composed by students and their manuscript music was difficult to read, which made my task seem even more onerous. Somehow I rose above my lack of experience with the result that the director of the conservatory asked me to join the staff to direct a new program for children.

That summer I went to New York for study. War clouds had been gathering even before I graduated from college and suddenly they hovered over my life. We in the Middle West had been inclined to believe they would never reach across the ocean but in the summer of 1917, they were shadowing lives all around us. I, too, felt their menace when I was called home two weeks before summer school was over. Reynold, my fiance, was scheduled to go overseas. I hurried home to tell him goodbye.

That fall I plunged into teaching the children keyboard harmony, ear-training, and rhythmic gymnastics. They were apt pupils and the rhythm classes, especially, kept me on my toes, literally and figuratively. I taught them to march note values with their feet while they expressed time values with their arms. I improvised rhythms at the piano making sudden changes in time and beat. It was a form of musical instruction quite new in our area and the children's recitals attracted much interest.

Some pageants were quite ambitious. Our "Mother Goose Ball" was repeated many times for town affairs and "The Fairies' Twilight Revels," performed outdoors at twilight with a professional orchestra furnishing the music, was a boon to war-weary audiences.

The fall of 1918 we began to hear rumors of an Armistice and when it actually occurred, our town, like the country itself, went wild with joy. After the whistles and bells had made the announcement, an impromptu parade was organized. Because I had impersonated the Statue of Liberty that fall in a patriotic benefit, I was called upon to ride on the dizzy height of a rather flimsily constructed float, holding my lamp aloft. I, who always shrank from high places and publicity in general, carried my light that morning with a singing heart. Reynold was coming home!

But he came home on a hospital ship. Reynold had been sent to an army hospital in Coblenz, Germany, with what the doctors called trench fever, but while he was there a lingering cough led to a more thorough examination and the doctors discovered that his lungs were affected.

It was June of the following year before he was well and released from the service. To satisfy both his parents and mine, Reynold had a thorough physical examination by our family physician and he was pronounced in good condition. We were married the following September. However, the following spring he contracted a bad cold and by June was once again in a veteran's hospital. Our future happiness was shadowed.

The conservatory asked me to produce another pageant that summer—a production that would be open to all the talented children in the community. Once again I was grateful for interesting work. It was produced in a large city park, an ideal setting for elves, fairies and wood nymphs who popped in and out among the trees to the strains of Grieg's "Hall of The Mountain King." The road was closed off and bleachers erected to take care of the three thousand spectators.

By the end of the summer, we realized Reynold was not improving. In fact, he was very ill and our family physician felt that hospital life was part of his trouble.

15

On the doctor's advice we moved across the country to a small health resort in California, hoping the change of climate would be beneficial.

In Monrovia two doctors were trying out a new cure for tuberculosis which entailed the placing of patients in homes (their own, if possible) and leaving the cure to rest, good food and fresh air, with only a minimum of nursing care. But even under such ideal conditions Reynold seemed, after three years of treatment, to be slowly growing worse.

Under the cloudless skies of California, I continued to stage pageants for civic organizations, lodges and schools. It was important that I work and I had grown to love the excitement and thrill of putting on a production, but trying to combine it with homemaking did create problems. I slept with a note pad and pencil on my bedside table since inspiration often came at night.

The six years that my husband was ill were difficult ones. We had "in-law problems" both ways. I could really understand my mother-in-law's reluctance to see us leave Iowa without her. She was sure she could have nursed her son back to health and was doubtful of my ability. Her fears did not add to my own small confidence. My own parents were sure I would come down with "consumption" and could see no reason why we were so headstrong as to want to carry the burden ourselves. I was welcome to stay on at home, but it was made very clear that my husband did not share that invitation.

Those were years of nurses, doctors and heartache,

too. Some days Reynold would be quite comfortable, but there were times when I faced the prospect of going on alone.

Perhaps, because of the difficulties, the uncertain future, the worry, we prized every moment that we were able to be together. On Reynold's good days he learned to play a mandolin (singing was against doctor's orders and he had a beautiful voice that he later used to sing professionally). We rented a rattly old piano and composed silly, popular songs by the hour. We were sure they would someday make us both famous and rich.

Preparing meals was simple. Reynold's were planned for him and the diet was rigid. The housework somehow seemed to do itself. There was no money for household help, but the little cottage the doctors had found for us was comfortable with a large sleeping porch for the invalid. I marvel now that we could have been so happy. We seemed to rise above our worries and live each day to the full . . . when our fears could be forgotten.

Too, those years were filled with work, real work, planning pageants and recitals and teaching pupils. Before I married, teaching had been fun. I was living at home during those two years that I taught at the Conservatory and my mother proved herself a capable secretary. She spent many hours at the telephone with lists I had made out—what costumes were to go to what group, what colors to which child. Now I was forced to plan every rehearsal, every costume, placate every doting mother (which was no small task). Homemaking certainly was a far cry from the way I had planned it.

I learned to appreciate my education. I learned the hard way the value and importance of a girl's being educated to earn her living. But real homemaking, creating a warmly welcoming place? There was none.

CAREER AND THE BABY

AFTER MY HUSBAND was restored to health and life became normal, I began to wonder if creative talent could really reach out in two directions. After our baby daughter arrived my home duties were almost doubled. Reynold, fortunately, did not resent my "other" life. He was very proud of my ability and appreciative of the help I had been able to give financially. It was rather an inner feeling of my own that in some way I was failing. I found myself begrudging the time that my work took me away from home. And when I was enjoying my home and baby a feeling of guilt would sweep over me with the conviction that I was neglecting the work I had been educated for. Such was the state of my thinking when a wonderful opportunity was dropped in my lap.

A local piano teacher (I had helped some of her advanced pupils with instruction in harmony and ear-training) had arranged for me to have a six weeks' course under a noted California composer. With indescribable joy, I immediately began to plan to take advantage of the lessons. I was to go to Los Angeles every morning five days a week for thirty lessons. I did have home obligations, but with my husband's cooperation they were solved. I obtained the help of a woman whom the baby knew and liked. She was a capable housekeeper so that my evenings at home were to be free from extra work.

The morning I was to leave I found myself actually wishing that opportunity had knocked more gently at my door. The living room, as I passed through, invited me to linger; the grand piano in the large front window beckoned me; the davenport and wing chair that I had slip-covered looked coolly comfortable this warm morning. (I recalled the day I had made those slipcovers and the care that had gone into the task. I had obtained the pattern and directions from a magazine and had followed the outline with minute care. Patty had supervised from her high-chair while I pinned and stitched.)

As I passed the baby's room, I paused to watch her for a moment. She was scolding her silver rattle and I longed to pick her up for a quick kiss but knew that would never do. I stood well back in the hall so that she could not see me, for I realized that a glimpse of Mama with her hat on might complicate matters for faithful Genevieve who at that moment had work to do in the kitchen.

"Why," I thought as I turned away, tiptoed off the front porch and hurried down the walk to the car, "do my two careers always seem to be at loggerheads?"

"What is the cause of all the frowns?" my husband asked as I slipped into the seat beside him.

"Nothing important," I said ruefully. "At least, nothing new. Just my two careers at each other's throats. When I'm keeping house I am well aware that my music is being neglected, and when I am at the piano or traveling off like this, the home and our child fairly cry out for attention."

At the newsstand near the ticket window I picked up a magazine to read on the hour's ride to the city. As soon as I was settled in my seat, I opened it at random and there, staring at me, was the title of an article that seemed italicized. "I Gave Up my Law Books for a Cookbook" were the words I read. Lucy R. Tunis began the article with a description of her first party, concluding with the apple pie that she prepared for her guests. When they complimented her and asked where she, a lawyer, had ever learned to make anything so difficult as a two-crust pie, she answered that she had learned how by studying law! In other words her ability to study and think through a difficult problem in her law office also worked for her in the kitchen. How many times, this same reasoning had stood me in good stead. After organizing and visualizing a pageant from beginning to end I found myself instinctively applying the same principle to a dinner party in my home.

She, too, had determined to have a real home "and no maid I could hire could give it to me," she said. Yet she had tried to continue with her law practice with the result: "My first, my principal interest was still, of course, the law." (And I myself had continued devoting my best thought to my job, too.) "Gradually," she wrote, "it came over me that the concentration necessary for the least possible household task was taking away my concentration upon my legal subjects." (How often I had felt just that way.) "Had I a job requiring no creative or personal strain, it might have been possible to go on doing justice to both jobs," she continued. And that same thought had occurred to me, too.

She asked a question which I had asked myself many times. "Should I go on and give my husband a makeshift home?" And she arrived at her decision with the same reasoning that had prompted mine: "I knew that some women expected their husbands to help, but if it affected my powers, would it not even more affect the powers of a man?"

She gave up her work to move to a location better suited for her husband's business. I had moved across the United States for the sake of my husband. But there the similarity in our adjustment to two careers ended. She had used her education to make a career of homemaking.

"I found that three years in a law office helped me to become a successful wife and homemaker," she wrote. "Indeed, the mental training I got there rather made up for the fact that I was not a natural born housekeeper and had no experience in that line." With these words she closed her case for the home.

Her trained mind was not *wasted* on homemaking, but was used to make her a success in a new career. The idea so stunned me that I sat upright, motionless, in my seat. Could one really reach contentment and, what was more, fulfillment by devoting oneself to just one career, by using one's talents to embellish and make lovelier one's home—instead of trying to balance the one or the other? What a challenge such a viewpoint presented.

I read and reread that article, with moments out for serious thinking, all the way to the city. Homemaking as a full time career I could well understand and accept, but to feel justified in sacrificing the work for which one was trained was a new idea. My heart told me it was a right one.

Some paragraphs from that article have stayed with me down the years. "All our ambitions are inspired by personal aims," she wrote. How often I have used this statement to measure my motives when ambition has suggested that I take on a new project. Now I ask myself, "Is this best for my home, for my family?"

Another statement that has brought me great comfort when I have felt the "pull" of activities outside the home is: "Whatever our calling and duty in life, it cannot be nobler than the creating of a home that is an inspiration to someone else."

By the time we reached the Los Angeles station, I was sure that this article had come to me for a definite purpose. My mind was made up. I called the conservatory, explained that I would not be enrolling in the course after all and was soon on my way home again.

On the return trip I built air castles—I dreamed of

how my new outlook was going to bless my home. I had always been afraid that without the incentive that my talents gave me, life might be boring. Now, I realized how wrong I had been. Homemaking, I knew, would always be a challenge.

I promised myself that I would be generous with these gifts of mine to help make my little world better. The small church we attended had asked me to play for the church services. Now I could see how easily I could take on that activity. And the schools were always needing help with their special programs. Oh, I would be busy, but I must use wisdom and keep these extra-curricular activities in their place—not allow them to take first place in my life again.

I knew from experience how dictatorial the talent of composition can be. It never had taken kindly to a time limit. In fact, it definitely rebelled at being turned on and off by the clock. I had composed a few sacred songs for my husband to sing at church, and I knew all too well how easy it was to lose all track of time when I involved myself in this hobby. I promised myself that I would lock away all manuscript paper, at least until Patty was old enough to be in school. I remembered with remorse the day that I had forgotten to give her lunch because I was so absorbed in a song I was writing. No more of that, I promised myself, firmly.

"But what if Reynold needs your help financially? What then?" I asked myself. And the answer came so easily to my awakened thought. "Be grateful that you can help. A few piano pupils will not interfere with your home if your motive is right—if you are simply doing your part to keep the home functioning. But be sure," my conscience warned me, "that you are not tempted to use your valuable time just to bring in silly little luxuries. Watch your values."

As we neared home I began to think of the baby—how her little hands would fly in the air when she saw me coming. And then I thought more soberly of Reynold. Would he understand? Or would he be disgusted at my changeableness? How could I explain this sudden impulse—this sudden change of plans?

I walked up from the station to the store where Reynold worked with a lagging step. He was waiting on a customer but the moment he saw me I knew everything was going to be all right. His face registered relief —yes, actually sudden relief!

"Am I glad to see you," he said. "Genevieve is having trouble with the baby. I was just getting ready to drive home and see what was wrong. The car is in the rear —help yourself and explain later."

How eagerly I ran up the steps to our front porch. Now, I knew I had been divinely led to return home and, too, I was perfectly sure that I had been promoted to a full-time career. I was content.

A MODERN MIRACLE

REYNOLD'S SUDDEN RECOVERY of health forty years ago was considered a miracle. Today it would not seem so strange, for Christian healing is now accepted by many churches as following in the footsteps of Jesus Christ.

Our interest in religion did not start with this experience. Before we were married we had decided that church affiliation was an important part of the home. We were young and not too thoughtful, but we did give enough consideration to religion to know that we wanted the church to be an integral part of our lives together. But that religion could become a part of our daily life never occurred to either one of us.

It was the third summer after we had moved to California for Reynold's health that religion really came into our lives. I had been teaching at the city's summer playground. Work, now, had become a real necessity. Often I dreaded leaving home. I usually asked a nurse or a friend to look in on my husband sometime during the day, for my hours at the playground were long. I realized Reynold should not be alone so much. Too, he had become so discouraged. He had hemorrhaged badly in the late spring and since then had been allowed no activity. His diet became even more restricted. He lived on shredded wheat and coddled eggs.

One day on my way home from work, a neighbor stopped to speak with me. Ivah often went in to cheer up the invalid especially when she knew my day was to be a long one. She and her husband were Iowans, too, and we had many mutual friends. On this afternoon, when she dropped in, Reynold barely acknowledged her greeting and she chided him for his lethargy. "Wig," she said, "you must make some effort yourself to get well." Her words at least aroused him for he answered her.

"I hope it will be over soon," he said. "The sooner I go, now, the better it will be for Floss."

Ivah was worried, fearing she had said too much. I tried to reassure her, but I climbed the steps to our cottage slowly, fighting tears and seeking desperately for control.

A few days before this incident, our pleasant landlady came to our door to tell us goodbye. She was leaving for a six weeks' holiday. Some of the discouragement I was feeling must have been evident because she returned in just a few moments and rather timidly offered me a little pamphlet called "Prayer and Healing" saying, "I'm sure this will help Wig if he will only read it."

I took the little article and thanked her politely (one doesn't offend one's landlady). I placed the pamphlet on Reynold's night table, saying, "Gypsy brought you this. You ought to read it, I guess." I don't remember that he even answered me.

About two weeks later, I came home one night and entered his room with the forced cheerfulness that had become a habit. Then, I stopped short just inside the door. The fever flush was gone from his face and the glassy brightness from his eyes. He even *looked* different, so at peace that I could not but marvel at the change. "What has happened?" I said.

"I don't know," Reynold said with an effort at a smile. "I read that little pamphlet just to get my mind off myself and it sounded so logical that I tried to pray. The pain left and so did the fever. I took my temp twice—shook it down, too, but it registered normal each time. Ever since, I've been afraid to move for fear I'll break the spell." And he grinned rather sheepishly.

"What do you *think* happened? Shall I call Dr. Kalb?" I said.

"No, oh no," he said. "Don't do that. I'm quite all right. Probably it was just time for the fever to break."

"Well, it has been time for that to happen for quite some time," I said. "Do you really suppose that reading you did has helped?"

"I don't know, except that I did gain a different idea of prayer than I ever had before. The little book said not only to beg for God's help but just to know that He is present, ready and waiting to be of help. It was a different idea of prayer than I ever had before and somehow God seemed very near. I was so comfortable all of a sudden. I was so at peace."

This sudden miracle, I felt, needed an explanation. I called a friend of our little landlady. After I told her what had happened, I said, "What do we do now?" She laughed heartily. "Just be grateful, my dear. But if you like, let me send a friend over to talk to you."

Reynold did not like the idea of the strange woman coming in the morning. He rather thought she might do something to "break the spell," as he said.

I argued with him and said if he would rather she did not come, I would bring the telephone to him and he could call her, but I thought we should find out a little more about this unusual experience. While we were arguing, the little lady knocked at our door. She was, as Reynold said, Whistler's mother in person, and how she read the Ninety-first Psalm!

There was no question but she well knew what every word meant. Her voice was softly and beautifully modulated; every word held deep meaning. And how she read it, beginning:

"He that dwelleth in the secret place of the most High shall abide under the shadow of the Almighty."

to the last beautiful verse:

"With long life will I satisfy him, and shew him my salvation" (Psalm 91:1, 16 KJV).

Every word was a beautiful prayer and we felt the very presence of the Father in that tiny room. Never before or since have I been so deeply moved.

From this time Reynold's progress toward health was steady, and life became normal in every way—but with a difference. The Bible became the most important and best read book in our home. We wanted to know how this healing had taken place. With humility we began to read and to study. Prayer took on new meaning for us as we began to realize it could be as effective now as when Jesus taught his disciples the prayer we call the Lord's Prayer—the prayer that covers all human needs. Prayer became a consciousness of God's loving presence, a realization that he knew our needs before we asked Him.

Too, we began to appreciate the importance of recognizing Jesus as the Christ, not just as a good man preaching on the hills of Galilee. We were impressed anew by Jesus' insistence that his Disciples recognize in him the healing Christ, His joy when Peter exclaimed, "Thou art the Christ," and His remarkable message to John, "Tell John what you have seen and heard; how that the blind see, the lame walk, the lepers are cleansed, the deaf hear, the dead are raised, to the poor, the gospel is preached." We began to comprehend that a loving God had sent His "only begotten Son" into the world to show the people of today as well as yesterday how to live richer, fuller, more useful, selfless lives.

While we had known much of this truth in a theoretical way, Reynold's healing made us realize how practical it could become in our every-day life. We felt we were being "born again" as we sought out religious source books to open our thought to the importance of the Master's every word and action. Gradually we became more and more conscious of God's presence and of the need to listen constantly for His voice, His guidance.

Our home was actually rebuilt on a faith in the goodness and love of an ever available Father. We began to turn to God for guidance in the simplest experiences of our everyday life. No longer a minor interest in the home, over night faith became life itself. We learned that faith must be built on the sturdy foundation of spiritual understanding. We pored over the healings of Christ Jesus that permeate the New Testament, for we had come to realize that He was our great Savior.

Faith seemed to come more easily to my husband than it did to me. After his healing he never doubted again. There were for me long months of waiting for that confidence, that child-like faith that is important. Even after I received proof, direct answers to my prayers, I was tempted to think they were coincidences.

By the time our baby daughter arrived I was turning more quickly and spontaneously to Divine Love for guidance. But I remember one experience when my new reliance was severely tested. Patty was not quite six months old. She had been fretful for a day or two when one morning she seemed very feverish. Her pitiable crying brought terror to me. Fear made me quite unable to think or to reason. I carried her in my arms all day and walked the floor in my anxiety. When Reynold came home from work that night he took the child from me and began to sing to her. That year he was soloist in the church we had joined and the song that he began to hum was the one he had sung in church the Sunday before. I knew it well, for I had rehearsed it with him many times. As he hummed I found myself following the tune with the words of the song which began:

What hast thou, O man, to fear?
Just know that Love divine is here.

Suddenly, my thought was flooded with relief. "Why, of course," I thought, "God is here, filling all space. God is the only Power there is and I know this is the truth." I burst into tears of relief as the fear that had been like a physical burden was completely lifted.

Patty was asleep before the song ended and slept well all that night. In the morning she was completely covered by a rash. A physician was called to comply with the health laws of the community, but he was frankly puzzled. It was a measles rash, he said, but no other symptoms were present. The baby was quite her happy self with no sign of fever. He decided to wait twenty-four hours before placing a quarantine and when he returned the following morning the rash had disappeared.

Children are very receptive and learn quickly to rely on God, and the mother who trusts her child to the Father's care is very wise. But one does have to be willing to say, "Father, this is Your child," and really mean it. When religion is *lived* in the home, trust comes more naturally and easily.

We as a family owe so much to that miracle of healing that came into our home so soon after it was established. Our family unity is due in a large part to the common bond that our understanding of and reliance on God has given us.

THE PORCELAIN CUP OF FRIENDSHIP

THE MEMORY of the wonderful friends who stood by us during the difficult days of Reynold's illness has sweetened and enriched our lives ever since. "The ornament of a house is the friends that frequent it," Emerson once said. While this is true, friends are far more than just the frosting on the cake; they are more nearly the life blood that keeps the home functioning in the community. The family that shuns all friendly contact with its neighbors, not only is breaking the Biblical commandment to love thy neighbor as thyself, but is denying itself opportunity to grow outward and, inevitably, into deeper communion with all mankind.

Before the automobile, when one packed a trunk for a fifty-mile journey, the arrival of guests was an event that created pleasurable excitement in the entire household. People valued communion with the outside world. Today the world is so much with us that at times we are inclined to retire to our castles and take up the drawbridge. Too often we entertain guests to return an obligation or to pay a debt rather than to enjoy the pleasure of company.

In our home we seldom entertain large groups of friends, except for open house and that is usually during the Christmas season. Then, the doors are literally open wide in Southern California, and it is an occasion we enjoy even more than do our guests.

When friends come for dinner the party is small. I found from experience that in a maidless, small home the hostess is then better able to enter into the fun and enjoy the party. Conversation is more relaxed and, usually, subjective.

During one evening that I like to remember, we discussed true friendship. Two dear friends were with us that night: Dotty, a warm-hearted woman who impetuously and generously gave of herself to her friends, and Henry, her husband, who was quite concerned about his wife, wishing she would give of her time and strength more wisely. That evening after dinner, I served the coffee in the living room before the open fire.

"Friendship is as fragile as this porcelain cup," Dotty said reflectively, almost ruefully, as she sipped her coffee.

I smiled at her sympathetically. I knew that only that very week she had been subjected to a disillusioning experience in the apparent desertion of a trusted friend.

Henry, across the room, nodded his head in quick

agreement as he set his cup carefully on the low table by his chair. "You're right, Dot," he said, "friendship is as fragile as good china and for that reason must be handled with utmost care. It should be for enjoyment rather than hard use."

Turning to me, he continued, "For months Dot has been at Margie's beck and call, waiting on her, running errands for her, taking care of her children. She even rented an apartment for her and attended to all the details of the moving!"

"Henry, you know Marjorie was practically paralyzed with fear from all those financial and domestic problems. She needed a friend—she needed practical help." Dotty defended her actions with spirit.

"It's just possible," Henry said thoughtfully, "that Marg did not want your help. Maybe she even considered you officious." Then to take the sting out of his words, he hastily added, "I can't help but think that your friendship cup cracked from too hard use."

"Good porcelain," I offered mildly, "is really quite strong. These cups were Grandmother's and came across the country in a covered wagon."

"And I'll wager they were packed with great care," Henry commented, with a quick grin for me.

"What about Jonathan and David?" Dotty asked. "Jonathan's friendship for David when he was in disfavor with Saul was certainly of real practical value."

Turning to my husband, Dotty spoke again. "What is your opinion, Wig? Do you think I broke my own friendship cup by too much use?"

My husband stirred the fire reflectively, and added another log before answering. "I've been thinking about that essay of Emerson's on friendship." Turning to me, he continued, "Do you recall what he said about having a friend? Didn't he say it was important to *be* one?"

"Let's take a look," I took down the well-worn volume of essays with its underlined passages and turned the pages quickly. "This will please you, Henry," I said and read aloud, " 'I do with my friends as I do with my books. I would have them where I can find them, but I seldom use them.' But then, there is this statement, Dotty, that Wig spoke of. It does substantiate your stand." And I continued, " 'The only way to have a friend is to be one.' "

Turning the page again, I read, " 'It has seemed to me lately more possible than I knew, to carry a friendship greatly on one side, without due correspondence on the other. Why should I cumber myself with regrets that the receiver is not capacious? It never troubles the sun that some of his rays fall wide and vain into ungrateful space, and only a small part on the reflecting planet. Let your greatness educate the crude and cold companion. If he is unequal, he will presently pass away; but thou art enlarged by thy own shining.' "

"Well, Henry, that just about says it all, doesn't it?" Reynold said with a laugh. "You should be happy, Dot, to have such a brilliant man on your side. Personally, I think your analogy between friendship and fine china is a good one. I understand that the finer the clay—the purer the ingredients it is composed of—the more beautiful the china will be. Its transluscence, as I understand it, is dependent upon the powdery whiteness, the purity of the clay."

"You think," I chimed in, "that Dotty's motives were so pure and selfless that she can expect her cup of friendship to be a lasting one?"

"That's the idea," my husband answered.

With a laugh, Henry added, "Just don't let hurt feelings, Dot, spoil the translucence of your cup."

"You needn't be concerned, if your cup isn't in constant use," I said. "When Grandma's cups are not needed, we just enjoy their beauty from the shelf in the corner cupboard. We know that when we want them they will be right there—ready and waiting."

My husband had the last word: "Your cup, Dotty, is not broken. Just put it on the shelf and keep it bright and shining. If Margie doesn't want it, someone else will."

There was a happy sequel to that evening's good conversation when, a few days later, Dotty called to say, "Apologies came my way today and thanks to our good talk the other night I was able to accept them with good grace. And," she added, "I do intend to keep my 'cup' bright and shining."

That week I had found a very helpful maxim of Benjamin Franklin's which I shared with her:

When befriended remember it;
when you befriend, forget it.

Together, Dotty and I had a good laugh for we both had learned a valuable lesson.

In adversity, which is the true test of friendship, we had an opportunity at one time to see good friends in action.

We awakened one morning to find the hill back of our home a mass of flames. Almost immediately we heard the siren and the radioed message telling us to move our cars into the street and prepare to leave on an instant's notice. For a moment I was in a state of panic. I felt rooted to the floor. As Reynold ran out the door to follow instructions and move the car, he called to me, "Phone Pat." That aroused me. She was alone, I knew, with her two babies, but she could pray for us and I knew that was what Reynold was thinking when he asked me to call. In a moment I was talking to her, explaining the situation. She offered to call a friend who had helped us many times with prayer and I left the phone calm, reassured and able to think clearly.

I remembered some friends who, the year before, had gone through a similar experience. Their home burned to the ground and in their panic they had left without even a photograph. At the time I had hunted through old albums of mine to find snapshots of their family to give to them—photographs of a mother who had left them, I remember, were so gratefully received. Profiting now by their sad experience, I went from room to room gathering up loved treasures that money could never replace. I had many framed photographs of both Reynold's parents and mine. Another, of my great, great-grandparents, was especially precious. In fact, one long wall in a hall was almost completely covered by these prized family pictures, most of them in quaint old-fashioned frames. These I quickly packed and then gathered up my scrapbooks—family-prepared genealogies and our loved college annuals. I looked longingly at Grandmother's rocker, her walnut bureau that had held her children's baby clothes and at Grandfather's desk, built for him by a valued friend in 1868. I snatched up a small handmade rug—my large wool ones that I had spent years braiding I knew I must leave behind. Grandmother's Haviland came next and I was still packing that, blinded a bit by tears, when an old friend appeared suddenly at the door.

The gates to the subdivision where we lived were guarded by the police. No one was allowed to enter. It was thought that curiosity seekers would interfere with the efficiency of the fire-fighters and with the evacuation if that became necessary. But a friend of long standing refused to accept this restriction. Perhaps, because he was well-known, he was at last allowed to enter on foot. He had trudged the mile to our home to lend us what help he could. How grateful we were to see his kind face. He and Reynold filled the car with the heavy boxes of dishes, but what was more important, he was there with his cheery smile and his moral support which we needed—badly.

Within a remarkably short time the wind suddenly changed direction and the danger was over, but the memory of this outstanding example of true friendship remains—warm reminders that the porcelain cup of friendship is never fragile but enduring and true.

George Washington gave sage advice in one of his letters: "Be courteous to all," he wrote, "but intimate with few; and let these few be well tried before you give them your confidence. True friendship is a plant of slow growth and must undergo and withstand the shocks of adversity before it is entitled to the appellation."

True friendship does grow slowly, but the friends we have accumulated down through the years have been lasting ones and have enriched our lives.

THE KITCHEN: HOME'S HEART

FRIENDSHIP and the kitchen have a strong affinity for each other. Most women who love to entertain keep an eye on the kitchen and a finger on its supplies so that they are never caught napping should an unexpected guest appear. Homemaking and hospitality are very close neighbors.

One spring, shortly before the fire that so nearly took our home, my husband had scheduled a concert in Pasadena, not far from our home. We were living in San Marino, and while our home was not large it was beautifully situated and we thoroughly enjoyed entertaining in an intimate way. The front lawn was ivy and the path to the street was a winding one meandering in a lazy way past a huge live oak tree that was supposed to be the oldest and largest one in the Pasadena area. There was a huge rose garden of seventy bushes at one side that kept the house decked with roses ten months of the year. A hedge of camellias could be depended upon to take over when roses were not available. All in all, we were a bit proud of this nest of ours and looked forward to entertaining our musically oriented friends. I began immediately to plan the refreshments but soon ran into a snag.

We had invited our friends, the Carmen Dragons, and the orchestra sponsor Joe Hoeft and his pretty wife Hazel among about twenty others. When Joe heard our plans, he insisted that it was far too much of an undertaking for me and took the party completely out of my hands. He hired a caterer and paid all the bills even to table decorations. It was a most generous gesture but somehow I no longer felt that it was my party and I felt depleted—disappointed.

The excitement that comes with the little special occasions always gives the true hostess a lift and keeps homemaking from slipping into dull, routine housekeeping. The alert homemaker recognizes that the kitchen is the true heart of the home.

During the depression there were times when our cupboard got pretty bare. I tried not to allow my close figuring to become too evident, but I seldom fooled the family. Pat was in High School during those years and one rainy night she came in just at dinnertime. The weather had been uncertain for several days and, aside from the economy aspect, I thought a crock of Boston baked beans would be appreciated. It had been my habit to stretch the food budget to the utmost toward the end of the month but this particular day was early in the month. As Pat stepped in out of the drizzle and cold she sniffed the air with appreciation as she said, "Is it the end of the month already?"

Somehow I liked to take tight places with a flourish. It gives me no end of satisfaction to triumph over emergencies. One evening at church, during those days of limited supplies, we ran into a whole carload of old friends whom we had not seen for many a day. Cordially, Wig insisted they come home with us for a "snack." I wondered most of the way home just what the snack would be—and then I remembered that Cousin Lynn in Iowa had just sent us our winter supply of popcorn. Popcorn and apples would be just the thing. And it was.

Keeping the house clean when help is difficult to obtain or pay for does present a hurdle. For a time we owned a two-story home and I was doing all the work myself. I worked out all kinds of schemes to keep myself at the task that I disliked so much. Kitchen work was fun, but dusting and sweeping and scrubbing took second place. The scheme that worked the best was a game I played often. "Just picture to yourself how your home would impress Mrs. So-and-so if she were to drop in this afternoon. You better get ready for her *quick.*" A childish game? Perhaps. But we all carry with us a few childish traits, I imagine.

A friend of mine who was so enthusiastic about many activities outside of her home that she never seemed to have time to keep her house in order, let alone cook a decent meal, once said to me apologetically, "You know, if my husband were hiring me to keep his house I'm sure he would have fired me long ago." And we do sometimes take advantage of our family's love for us.

Too, I have wondered if, perhaps, poorly cooked meals may not be one important reason for the ascending divorce rate. The way to a man's heart is said to be through his stomach. It just might be wise to give a little more consideration to what goes into it.

To be a good cook it is important to start out with at least the desire to achieve that goal. I had two grandmothers and a host of aunts who were superior cooks and, with their recipes in my pocket and a vivid memory of how things should taste, I never allowed myself to accept defeat.

Armed with a good basic cookbook, a woman has no excuse for continuing indefinitely to be a poor cook. But no one who wishes to shine in the kitchen should limit herself to one book of recipes, no matter how good it is. I have a long shelf of excellent books and I add to it constantly. Each one has something special to offer and not the least ingredient to look for is inspiration. In *Strawberry Point Kitchens* I make a suggestion that is invaluable—make your own recipe file. Every time you have a recipe given you that you especially prize, record not only the recipe but the name of the friend who gave it to you. These homemade cookbooks are a treasure for they remind you of the friend, the home, and the pleasant occasion when you first tasted the recipe. Usually I add little comments about the circumstances under which I obtained it, thus fortifying my memory of the occasion. Until you try this suggestion and build your own cookbook, you will never realize what an inspiration such a culinary history can be for your morale as a cook. If inspiration is present, one can be sure that the food will be good to the taste, beautiful to the eye, and what is also important, it will be fun to prepare.

A number of good cookbooks is a great help, too, in keeping variety the important spice in the kitchen. I love to compare the same recipe in different books— the way the ingredients are handled. How, for instance, does Fannie Farmer's way with baked beans differ from Irma Romberg's in *Joy of Cooking?* Irma uses dark molasses and includes catsup in her recipe, baking the beans slower. Fannie uses twice as much molasses and specifies "light," omitting the catsup, which is more to our taste. But I prefer the slower baking of the other recipe. In just this way it is possible to combine parts of one recipe with parts of another and often one experiences the thrill of inventing a new recipe!

I have one book that I keep just for my hurry-up meals. And it is a dandy. I must say that I shut my eyes to the wines suggested at the foot of every dinner in the book, for we do not approve of liquor in any form in our home, even for cooking. This book, Marian Meade's *Modern Homemaker,* has one chapter devoted to most unusual sandwiches, and the appetite provoking pictures that accompany the recipes are an important feature.

It may seem odd, but even old-time cooks have moments when it is a distinct advantage to have a modern-day cook at her elbow with one of her short-cut methods immediately available.

Another book, to go from one extreme to another, is the story of housekeeping on a Michigan farm. *The Country Kitchen* by Della Lutes is now out of print, I am sorry to say, but some libraries still carry it. I find its homey atmosphere and quaintly worded recipes a joy. Published in 1935, it was reprinted almost every year until 1955. It is full of recipes that bring to mind the wonderful farm kitchens of a generation ago.

Every woman who puts her kitchen on the priority list of household interests will find her own short-cuts to good, nourishing meals—short-cuts that are always influenced by her love for and the needs of her own family. She can also find rich food for her mind in memories of recipes from special friends and occasions. This "heart of the home" is all-important.

FOOD FOR THE SPIRIT

MEALS that are well-planned and well-served surprisingly provide excellent food for the spirit. When the machinery of housekeeping is well-oiled and meals appear like magic, then breakfast as well as dinner becomes an occasion that the family looks forward to. Somehow, someway, a miracle takes place and some of the fruits of the spirit—gentleness, joy and love—are in evidence. Conversation, spiced with such virtues, is bound to be relaxed and happy.

To create the illusion of effortless meals is no small achievement in today's maidless home. It does take careful thought and planning—the kind we all give instinctively when guests are expected. But a candlelit table, a rested, relaxed homemaker and a delicious, well-cooked meal are a combination appreciated by a family as well as by guests.

Some homemakers who are careful how food is prepared—that it is appetizing and tasty—are careless how it is brought to the table unless guests are present. But is there a guest anywhere in the world who means as much to a woman as her own family? Or is more deserving of a candlelit table and fresh linen? Aren't our loved ones worth fussing over?

Good meals do not just happen. We all know that the greater the artist, the more effortless the art, whether it is painting, singing or dancing. The same rule holds true when the artist is a homemaker. Thought and more thought must go into every detail of the planning and serving if we want every meal to be not only an artistic success but true food for the spirit.

Recently, my daughter and I discussed this very subject as we lunched together downtown.

"Really, Mother," Pat said, "you must admit that with all the time-saving inventions of today, meal-preparation does not need such careful planning. Women do have much more time than you did a generation ago. That is why we can take on so many outside activities."

"Yes?" I said with a question mark in my voice. "I thought there were still twenty-four hours in the day."

"But think of the short-cuts we now have," Pat said, and I am sure there was amusement in her voice. "We not only have good trick foods but trick clothes as well. The new materials have made laundry no problem."

"Granted," I said. "But very few of you young housewives have the help in the home that my friends and I took for granted a generation ago. You do all your own work as do most of your friends. Electric servants still have to be manipulated and that takes time. Your days, too, have to be well planned or you end up at the delicatessen shop at 5:30 in the afternoon and rush madly home to slap together a hurry-up meal. I know. There were delicatessen shops when I was young, too."

"But, Mother, we do have so many more demands upon our time. Many of our outside activities are important, especially the help we give the schools. Don't you think they justify simpler meals?"

"It is for you to decide, of course. But you are mistaken if you think mothers did not have outside interests when you were little. From the time that you were eight until you were eleven, I obligated myself for important church work that took three hours of daily study. I just planned my household tasks around it and I am sure you and your father did not suffer. No, Pat, it isn't that you have more time or more activities than I had. It is simply a matter of how you use your precious hours and how you plan them."

"Mornings are the hardest," Pat said, with a sigh. "Everyone is in such a hurry."

"Did you ever try setting your breakfast table at night? Aunt Emma always did. She claimed it was a great help. Do you allow time at the breakfast table for the Bible lesson and a short prayer? They are food for the spirit, you know."

"Not any more. Now the children read by themselves in their rooms," Pat answered.

I shook my head. "That reading is important, too, but it doesn't take the place of family reading and family prayers. They supply you with a *united* spirit that fortifies all of you for a day in the world. Don't neglect it," I said with a smile, as we parted company.

The secret, if you wish to call it that, is planning and a great deal of quiet thought. A restful, comfortable home does not just happen—it must be sought for. The atmosphere of the home is really the wife's responsibility. It is her duty to see that desirable qualities are expressed there. The home is the reflection of her own thinking.

There are two desirable qualities that we seldom credit with influencing the atmosphere of the home but both of them are tremendously important in providing food for the spirit. Both of them come to us from generations of good homemakers but with proverbs attached. Perhaps that is the reason we are inclined to take them for granted. We, in our youth learned to glibly say, "Order is heaven's first law" and, "Cleanliness is next to godliness" but familiarity has deadened the message. Certainly we intend our homes to express both order and cleanliness, but we seldom think how important they are in regard to the harmony of the home.

When I was a young bride an older friend whose home always expressed the restful quality of order confided that each night after the family retired she made a tour of the house to see that everything was in its place. "There must be a place for everything and everything must be there," she added, "if you want your home to be a little bit of heaven."

Cleanliness in a home is apt to be taken care of at regular intervals and on a working schedule, but order is more or less subject to the events of the day. To the woman who prides herself on keeping peace and harmony in her home, it is important that she look well to the orderliness of her household.

The three years that I was devoting three hours a day to important study, I found a working schedule for meals was an important help in keeping a smooth-running home. I discovered that my menus for a week followed a rather set plan. The meats, especially, followed a pattern that did not vary too much—a roast, a steak or chops, one cheaper cut and a meat substitute usually. By buying for the week I saved valuable time. The meats set the tone of the meals and with that taken care of, it was a simple matter to order the accompanying vegetables and fruits.

One list which has been most helpful in saving time is my catalogue of staples of household needs. There are about thirty items which are important to keep on hand at all times. A quick glance at the staple list before I leave on a trip to market often saves another trip.

Meals for special occasions, particularly when they are party events, need special consideration. With this need in mind I created still another scrapbook and it has been a tremendous help in planning such affairs. It is a large, three-holed notebook and is filled with sixty pages of pictures from favorite magazines.

The first pages of this "party book" are filled with photographs of mouth-watering canapés and party dips. These are followed by pages of pictures of open house parties. Just to see the tall, frosted glasses of colorful drinks and the huge punch bowl floating slices of orange on its ruby depths is to feel a party mood fast approaching.

Tea tables ready for New Year's callers make another interesting picture. On the same page a late supper table with a chafing dish and a waffle iron awaits the after-theater guests.

Still another page (and this one I consult often) is devoted to attractive tea trays and tea tables. The words accompanying the pictures create a desire to call in one's friends to share a cup of tea. I always get the urge for a party when I thumb through this homemade picture book. Whether I am planning an Easter brunch, a Valentine luncheon or a Mayday tea, I can always find the inspiration I need in my party book.

When we were first married Reynold and I determined we would always dress up a little for dinner. Enough of that good intention stayed with us so that we do make the dinner hour a little special. We do not always eat in the dining room. We find it is fun to eat all over the house—sometimes on the porch or patio, sometimes at a bridge table in front of a roaring fire in the living room. Sometimes (not too often) in the study in front of the television screen when a special program attracts us. But for a real dinner, we usually come back to the dining room and then we present ourselves dressed up for the occasion. And we try to dress up our thinking, too. The family does not need to know how much organization and planning has gone into a seemingly simple meal. The man of the house seldom brings home the problems of his busy day. Neither does the housewife need to explain the inner workings of her well-ordered home.

Our conversation at dinner naturally is inspired by our happiness in being together—in sharing the interesting events of our day. Mealtime is usually the only time in the day that the family is able to meet and it should be a leisurely time, an hour of food for the spirit, of family at-one-ness. And if the lovely old custom of asking God's blessing on the household is observed, His tender presence will be felt.

A PENNY—SAVED AND SPENT

BOTH THE SPIRIT and the vision of the home are quickly dampened if the proper respect is not paid to what Paul, in his famous letter to Timothy, designated as "the root of all evil." However, it is well to remember that it is the *love* of money rather than money itself that Paul is warning of. Perhaps its misuse would more accurately describe the problem it has become today. Many authorities, upon examining the causes for friction in the home, have given priority to this very subject— money and its misuse.

Often it is not the large sums of money that cause the problems in a marriage, but the "little foxes that spoil the vines." The small monetary leaks may seem unimportant at the time they occur, but they eat away the confidence in one's marriage partner. (There is a tendency in all of us to blame someone or something else when income does not meet outgo.)

Perhaps, because I was the bread-winner during the early years of homemaking, the running of the financial budget became my responsibility. From conversations with friends, I judge that this "burden" was, in reality, a blessing. The homes that I know well, where the wife runs the pocketbook, seem to sail the financial seas with fewer shipwrecks. Certainly, there is less rocking the boat than when both senior members of the household try to handle it together.

In our home we tried for many years to adapt the needs of the household to "prepared" budgets and our good intentions always ended in disaster. Fitting individual needs into suggested, specific pigeonholes gave us nothing but trouble. I often found myself by the end of the month robbing Peter to pay Paul.

Now, once a year, I make out what I call my "minimum budget." It scales down the "outgo" to an amount of money that is just enough to maintain self-respect. With my years of managing on a slim budget, this has not been difficult to do. Little money is actually necessary to finance a modest home if one is honest in his appraisal of the "needs and wants" of the household.

My own parents, who themselves would never have entertained the idea of budgeting, used just such a plan. When I was a child I was taught to ask myself before I indulged in a purchase, "Do I *need* this, or do I just *want* it?" Very often my honest answers did not please me. (There were times when I would have preferred hyacinths to a loaf of bread.)

My parents built a new home in the early 1900's and the question of "needs and wants" was the subject of nightly debates for many weeks. Those were the days when no self-respecting man had a mortgage on his home. This fact, I am sure, influenced my parents' decision not to paper the upstairs rooms. We endured the cold, white walls for two years until the disgraceful mortgage was paid in full.

In those days, too, there were no "time purchases." I remember well the first time I ever heard of such an arrangement. A young sister of my mother wanted a piano and she bought it "on time." My father's red hair stood on end. "If she could not save the money in advance, how did she expect to save it after the thing was bought?" he asked. "Besides she paid twice what it was worth," he added. Profiting by my loved aunt's experience, I saved diligently for two years to buy my parlor grand. I knew it would never have been allowed in the house if it had not been paid for in full.

With my background of respect for careful expenditures, the idea of a "minimum budget" appealed to me. Then came the interesting part—the dividing of the remainder of the income into two equal parts. (Or if the income fluctuates, I use the former year as my standard to work from.) One half of the money becomes the basis for a saving program. The other half I return to the "minimum budget" that I have already established. How rich it makes one feel to see the standard of living rise over night to a comfortable level!

Perhaps an example of how this works would be helpful. If a family has an income of, say, $1000 a month and has established a minimum budget of $300, there would be $700 left to divide equally between a more comfortable living plan and a well worked out savings program. With $350 added to the minimum budget, the living expenses will be assured of $650 on which to take care of family needs. The savings program of $350 would constitute the family's backlog of protection. This would include not only an insurance program but emergencies that arise from time to time in the best regulated homes.

By dividing the income as suggested and setting aside a generous amount for emergencies, one faces the unexpected with equanimity. The real value of the plan is, of course, a mental one—the knowledge that living expenses will not eat up the full salary check—that the family is not *limited* to $650 for living expenses, but that it is *free to enjoy* this comfortable standard of living knowing that both emergencies and savings have been provided for.

One important principle that we adopted about that time has to do with benevolence—its importance in any well-balanced family plan. We made it a "controlling account," even to the point of giving consideration to the Biblical precept of the tithe law as outlined in the book of Malachi. Father Wiggins, who was a Congregational minister, used to say, "you don't start giving until you have paid your tithe." And due to Reynold's miraculous healing, we found expressing gratitude in this way came to us easily.

I remember one Saturday morning soon after he was restored to health that Reynold came to me to ask if I would mind if he gave all the money we had in our little bank account to the church the next morning. There were no more classes on the horizon until fall and it was over a week before he would receive his meager government check. I took a deep breath and said, "Go ahead." The next morning our check was in the collection plate. Sunday evening a woman I knew slightly called me from a nearby town to say that she and her husband belonged to a little club and the group would like to take a course of lessons from me. They would like to start the next evening! I came home from that class with far more money than we had given to the church. At first we considered this experience just a happy coincidence, but time has proved to us that when the heart is right, such experiences are not a happenstance.

The wise use of money indicates, I think, the character of an individual. Certainly, it is true that not money, but the love of it (the disproportionate use of it), is the "root of all evil."

GATHER 'ROUND TO SING A SONG

TODAY an important item in the family budget is music. Not only the expensive television set but phonographs, radios and tape recorders are considered necessities if we are to bring music to the home. And yet, how seldom music is expressed by the family in this well-equipped home. Talent today must be professional, it seems, to be accepted.

Music in the home was all important, too, at the turn of the century. But if we did not make it ourselves we did not have it—not until after the phonograph (really the graphaphone) put in its appearance in our small Iowa town. As the little black cylinder revolved and the music came forth from the morning glory horn, we sat entranced.

The gramaphone was a significant step in the mechanization of music and it also signaled the departure of self-made music from the home. Until the day when we heard Sousa's famous band, we were quite content with our own performance.

The change was not sudden. We continued to enjoy

the music we made ourselves for quite some time, but we were no longer entirely dependent upon our own efforts for musical entertainment.

By the time the Victrola appeared and recordings of famous artists were available, the piano definitely had begun to lose popularity. It was still considered a necessary piece of furniture in any well-furnished home but it was by then quite overwhelmed by the new invention.

For a few more years all little girls continued to take "music" lessons, but enthusiasm for becoming proficient on the instrument was lacking. Social life was not limited to playing charades, making fudge or gathering around the piano for a sing. By the second decade of the twentieth century young people were rolling up the rugs to dance to the music of the now excellent phonograph. In another decade it was the radio with its "live" music and, then, television. By that time the piano had been relegated to the attic or traded in for a stereo.

I do not mean to imply that the youth of our country ceased singing with the demise of the piano. Other instruments have contributed to the song-fests of youth for generations and probably always will. These young adults have been quite independent of the mixed-age group that for so long gathered around the piano. Whenever or wherever they congregated by themselves, in the exuberance of youth, they wanted to sing and they did. While their choice of music as well as instruments did not always win the approval of their elders, they continued to follow their own star right down to the present day—both in the choice of instruments they use for their accompaniments and in the songs they sing.

Even while the piano still dominated the parlor, the young people were dedicated to both ukeleles and ragtime when they congregated on porches or for picnics, much to the disgust of their ballad-loving parents. They, in their time, had devoted many hours to "Love's Old Sweet Song" and the gentle accompaniment of a softly strummed guitar. (Its electrically manipulated counterpart has now moved into the realm of "classical" music and is no longer limited to chording accompaniments.) Youth's devotion to the fad of the moment —even the strange rock of today—is not cause for concern. It changes with each generation. What we should regret is the loss of a valuable family custom.

In the few homes where the piano still holds an honored place and is used for holiday and evening "sings," a warm bond of togetherness is felt.

Whenever members of a family share a common interest they enjoy each other. And the creation of music is one interest that is almost universally enjoyed. Everyone loves to sing if he or she will only admit it. What our country needs is more amateur musicians—people who do not aspire to professional status and are content to use their talent to make their homes warm and attractive and to enrich everyday living.

So often we hear the excuse, "I don't have a talent big enough to warrant cultivating." Such an excuse always reminds me of the Biblical parable of talents—even though they are a different kind of talent. The man, you remember, distributed his talents among his servants and returned later to find that the lad who had received only one had buried it to preserve it. Talents grow with use. Not many of us have the desire or the ability to be a Rubinstein, but there is no reason to deny ourselves the pleasure—yes, the *pleasure* of making music and creating a musical atmosphere for the family.

We are too much a nation of hero-worshippers. In Europe, especially Italy, this is not true. The men and women from the humblest walks of life know *good* music and how they love to sing, hum, whistle. We like to be informed but we are diffident about claiming excellence for ourselves. It is as though we fear we shall seem pretentious and be embarrassed in the process. Such an attitude is wrong—so wrong. What if we are mediocre? What if our taste is plebeian? If we like only popular music let's not be afraid to admit it.

The Boston Pops concerts have done a great deal to start people toward a sincere enjoyment of good music, while they listen to the simpler classics in the process. What is true of listening is also true of performing. The person who gives up the piano because he feels inadequate to perform Chopin's études is punishing himself needlessly.

Music takes us where it finds us and if we are brave enough to restore the piano to our living rooms and learn to play it or brush up on our childhood lessons we shall be well repaid. No phonograph or radio or television can establish the intimacy and charm of the music

63

we make ourselves and particularly the music we play with others. And this includes singing, too, of course.

Too many of us have denied ourselves the pleasure of making music because we do not trust our own taste. But the more we play, the sooner our taste improves. If music appeals because of the beauty of sound, or because it stirs our emotions, or because of the gaiety of a syncopated rhythm, then let's enjoy it that way. Rhythm happens to be the gate through which I enter. Intellectual stimulation may come later. In the meantime, let's begin—just where we are.

The family that enjoys expressing its love of song by gathering around the piano should never feel apologetic. We are very foolish to give up a single custom that has proved to be a pleasure to past generations. My grandparents enjoyed the old singing school with only a pitch pipe to start them off. My parents, also, attended these sings. By the time I arrived, my mother had earned for herself a black ebony piano, one of the very few pianos in our small town. (Organs were numerous but not pianos.) The friends interested in making music naturally gravitated to our parlor and those pleasant evenings are among the happiest memories of my childhood.

The songs they sang reflected our nation's growth. Some of them dated back to the very founding of our country when we were still a colony. Some expressed the fiery spirit of our great Revolution; others recalled the bitter years of slavery and the war that opposed it. The "new" songs of my parents' time were sentimental ballads and were the first to be published as "sheet" music. Charles K. Harris was perhaps the best known of all sheet music writers. In his lush office in Milwaukee was a sign that read:

Charles K. Harris
Banjoist and Song Writer
Songs Written To Order.

Many of them did sound "written to order" and many of them deservedly have not survived but those that have lived have become a part of our nation's heritage. We still sing "Daisy Bell" (more popularly known as "A Bicycle Built for Two"), "In the Good Old Summertime" and "In the Shade of the Old Apple Tree." "Listen to the Mocking Bird" was a favorite with my parents, but it was written during the Civil War. It is said that people danced to its strains on the White House lawn when the news of Lee's surrender was received.

The songs of the country before 1776 include many hymns that are to be found in hymn books today. "Old Hundred" was in a book of hymns that came with our Pilgrim fathers from Holland. In England, Isaac Watts broke away from psalm singing by producing such hymns as "O God Our Help in Ages Past." Not all of the first century immigrants were Puritans and Pilgrims. The Germans in Pennsylvania and the English who settled the Virginias and the Carolinas were singing people and their songs are with us still. Martin Luther gave his people the famous hymn, "A Mighty Fortress is Our God," and John Wesley gave the people of South

Carolina the lovely "Jesus, Lover of My Soul."

In my childhood I remember that hymns were an important part of every evening of song. The rich four-part harmony they seemed to demand made them an important addition not only to an evening's sing but to the family reunions of those days. Because of the happy memories associated with such evenings, I made music an important family custom in my own home. Now our daughter is continuing the same pleasant tradition in her home.

Because we did not stress the idea of special talent, our daughter learned to love music for itself and learned to play the cello as well as the piano. Very often, I have noticed that when unusually gifted children are "pushed" by ambitious parents to become prodigies, when old enough to make their own decisions, the children not only abandon the instrument they played well but music in general. Reynold and I did not want that to happen and happily it did not. Pat married a man who loves music too, and Sunday evenings in their home are very often given over to home-made music.

These young parents are instilling a love for music in their children who are, even now, beginning to take an active part in the family programs. Little Chad has an excellent sense of rhythm but has not progressed much beyond a duet of chop-sticks with his sister. But twelve year-old Candi plays the piano with all the finesse of an adult. The flute, too, interests her and she is hoping to soon be playing first flute in the school band.

Sometimes on Sunday evenings she relinquishes the piano to Grandmother and we have a trio of cello, flute and piano with the men of the family singing along as we play familiar tunes. Recently a newfangled organ has joined the family circle. Chad and his father take turns and are having great fun playing by letter and color.

One of the fallacies in regard to learning music is the notion that if one has never been exposed to it as a child it is practically impossible to achieve any skill. It is, of course, an advantage to have had an early start but it is quite possible to attain a measure of proficiency in later years. To introduce music into a home takes initiative on someone's part—someone has to say, "Let's do it." Usually it is the mother who suggests this family project. If she has never been exposed to music she need not accept defeat. New methods have simplified the process remarkably. Books have been prepared for the adult student and they take the beginner a long, long way in a remarkably short time—a matter of a few weeks. I perhaps should warn the neophyte that hymns are just about the most difficult music to play when one has had very little experience in reading music. Simple folk melodies that everyone knows are simpler to start with.

With Mother at the piano it will be no time before family music will begin to shape up. It is the doing—the actual playing or singing that is important. Before you know it, you will be singing four part harmony and playing acceptable chamber music. Then, open the door to the neighbors. Don't make apologies. Just remember this is for fun. Say with Emily Dickinson, "I'm nobody! Who are you? Are you nobody, too?" And then, without pretense, add: "Come over tonight for supper and be sure to bring your violin."

TRAIN UP A CHILD

THE PARENTS who are seeking guidance in rearing a family will find their best help in a Book that never grows old or out of date. The Bible is full of interesting stories that deal with various problems of discipline. Solomon, whose wisdom is ageless, offered the excellent advice: "Train up a child in the way he should go and when he is old he will not depart from it." Psychiatrists, I understand, are in complete agreement with Solomon. They hold the opinion that between the ages of three and six, children establish the basic pattern of behavior that they will follow the rest of their life. It is well to realize the importance of the early years in child training.

It is not surprising that a mother who is young and capable of earning a good salary or carrying on an absorbing career finds it difficult to see why she should expend that talent at home when it is possible to park her healthy offspring in a well-recommended nursery school. The woman in charge may be better able to "train up a child" than is she, the child's mother. But that is not the important issue. The price she will pay for those lost years with her baby is far too high unless necessity forces such a decision.

But nursery schools do have their place and often fill a need even for the stay-at-home mother. When Patty was about three, I realized she needed to be with children her own age. She simply did not know how to play. The children in the neighborhood were older and loved to humor her. The price of a nursery school was not in my budget, but I visited a school anyway to make inquiry. I found the teacher needed a pianist to play for the children's games, so throughout that lovely summer Patty had friends and I enjoyed the change, too.

Early training is mostly the building of character. The Bible was our big help in this. In fact we were educating ourselves right along with our daughter. One verse that was a big help we called the "whatsoever verse." It is in Paul's epistle to the Corinthians where Paul names all the virtues we are "to think on"—things "true," "honest," "just," "pure," "lovely," and of "good report." As we tried to express these qualities ourselves it was natural for our child to follow our lead. The "good report" was especially important, we thought. How easy it is to bring in the "tattle-tale" stories whether we are six or sixty. We found these good qualities were better lived than talked about—too much anyway.

Parental love wisely tempers discipline. Somehow, a child recognizes that it is administered with love and accepts it. We witnessed a good example of the influence of parental love in our own family. Randy, our small nephew, was such a dynamo of energy that his relatives almost dreaded his visits to them. His poor mother, worn out by his excessive good spirits, gladly turned him over to his father for discipline and guidance. Secretly we felt that Harry was far too easy on the child. He never raised his voice, always kept his cool, and was just quietly there every moment, until we really felt he was giving far too much of his life to the rearing of this child.

As the years added up, the companionship between father and son grew stronger until their interests did actually become the same. Now, Randy is a model young man in second year college. He is working part-time to pay his way and at the same time learning a business he plans to make his life's work. He is so emotionally well adjusted that he is popular with both boys and girls in his crowd and best of all he and his father are still close friends and plan their vacations together. Solid is the only word for Randy and now we all are very proud to claim him as our kinsman.

Children are really much happier when well-disciplined—when they know what is required of them. They are not only happier but more at ease if their early training points out the do's and don't's of the household. To know what is expected of one and why, gives even us adults a sense of order and direction.

One way my grandchildren have been made aware of their duties and obligations to the welfare of the home has been through charts. I see them clipped to the refrigerator door in the kitchen. I'm not sure how they operate, but I think the children gain credits for tasks well done. There are points for promptness and penalties when they are amiss. I know there is very little talk about these duties. I never hear their parents scolding or calling attention to these tasks. The children seem to have learned that it is up to them whether or not they qualify for the rewards or the penalties.

Grandparents make very few constructive contributions to the training of their children's children. They are wise if they look the other way when discipline is being administered, for they are much too soft-hearted where grandchildren are concerned. They should have the fun of watching the growth of these budding thoughts but none of the responsibilities. I live near my daughter and her family and being a part of the family circle gives me great joy. I agree heartily with Margaret Mead when, in her recent book *My Earliest Years,* she says, "What our society lacks today is the mutual beneficial closeness between grandchildren and grandparents. Grandparents give you a sense of how things were, how things are." (How my two grandchildren love to look through my 1911–1915 scrap books and draw comparisons.) Children do indeed need three generations to grow up with.

One thing that cements the feeling of "togetherness" in the family is religious education. Parents who guide their children's spiritual ideals are very wise. The forces of evil are leveling a vicious attack at family life today and a family with a religious background is fortified to resist the assault.

When Patty started school we formed the habit of reading a Bible lesson and having prayer each morning at the breakfast table and the child soon learned to depend upon it to start her day right. At that time her father was singing professionally and for three years he was the soloist in a large church forty miles from home. Since the Sunday services were morning and evening and there was one other service on Wednesday evening we soon rented a small furnished apartment so that we could stay over between services on Sunday and stay all night on both Sundays and Wednesdays. Very often our mornings were a bit hectic, for we had to drive home before school convened at nine o'clock. One morning when we were especially tardy and were driving against time, we heard a plaintive voice from the back seat, "Won't we get home in time for the lesson?"

Her father answered quickly, "We don't need to wait until we get home. If Mother will get the Book we'll have our lesson right now as we ride along." And that we did. I brought out the Bible from our overnight bag and read the lesson as we drove along. Patty and I had our silent prayer and we all repeated our little daily prayer and the Lord's Prayer together, Daddy joining in. After that we often depended on the ride home to establish us in right thinking for the day.

Children are born mimics. If we wish them to be polite, considerate, unselfish and, in short, well-mannered, we shall do well to practice these virtues ourselves. How often we hear it said of the small lad who strides along, trying to match his stride to his father's, "How manly he is, just like his father." And of his sister, as she graciously greets a guest, "Like mother, like daughter."

While we no longer give credence to the familiar quotation, "Children are to be seen, but not heard," we often fail to give the attention to the ideas our little people bring to us that they deserve. We resent being interrupted when we are speaking, but do we offer the same courtesy to the children in our home?

I often think of the small niece of a friend of mine. She had an older sister who was inclined to put words in her small sister's mouth. The little one's vocabulary was not quite equal at times to the thoughts that were demanding expression. One day when she was searching for words to relate to her mother an exciting experience, her older sister interrupted, saying, "What she means, Mother—" But on this occasion she, herself, was interrupted. With brown eyes flashing and a quick stamp of her little foot, the youngest voiced her long pent-up complaint, "You can't think my 'thinks' for me." How often we are tempted to think other people's *thinks* for them and how frustrating such interruptions can be—for children as well as for adults.

With school, problems for parents will take on a different hue. Certainly our public schools need the intelligent help of parents now more than ever before in the history of our country. Education is not what it should be. Many remedies are being offered and perhaps the best one is to retrace our steps for a generation or two, back to the schools that fostered the fundamentals in education.

One mother in Southern California made a plea in a newspaper a year or so ago for smaller schools. She feels that the children need a "good, small neighborhood school. Small enough for parents to know the teachers and feel that they really care about the children."

One thing that parents can do is to see that children in the home are encouraged to *desire* a good education; they can be encouraged to read good books and to appreciate them. Reading aloud, too, should be encouraged.

One big step of progress in the last one hundred years is the equal education of girls and boys. But parents need to be especially alert to help these well-educated girls find their rightful place in the complicated world of today.

Girls are now brought up to realize they are just as smart, just as capable as their brothers but if they wish to enter the business world they suddenly find that it is still a man's domain. No wonder the young woman of today feels "put-upon." And this is where the home once more comes importantly into the picture.

If our daughters are brought up to realize they are not only as intelligent and capable as our sons, but that they have *added* abilities that boys can never compete for, then they will recognize that they are singularly *blessed* in being women. Instead of competing with their brothers, girls should be taught to cultivate those added qualities they possess if they would be well-balanced women with happy, well-organized homes.

I speak from experience when I say that Longfellow's words are still very true—"home-keeping hearts are happiest." It would have been very easy for me to have carried on a personal career after being the bread-winner of the family for three years but, as I related in an earlier chapter, I knew that such an arrangement would have weakened my husband and that our home would be happier if I did not deprive him of his right to provide for his family.

Parents can stress the importance of the woman in the home and help their daughter realize that it is her domain and the basis of her happiness. She must be taught to value it, to treasure it, to bring all her talents to bear upon making it a success and the center of family life. Her developed talents will always make her a more interesting individual and companion and they are a back-log for emergencies. (I was very grateful to be able to earn my living and support our home when my husband was so ill.) *But* let men reign supreme in the business world. Why should a woman wish to take from her husband the manly ability to provide for his family? It is as natural for him to wish to support his home as it is for her to center her happiness there. Equal education should create equal spheres of activity, but they need never interfere with each other.

Yes, train up a boy to be manly, to take pride in his masculine heritage, but train up a girl to be equally appreciative of her femininity, her womanliness. And when they are old, as Solomon so wisely said, they will not depart from these virtues, and they will rise up and call their parents blessed.

THE NEW WOMAN

"MANY MOTHERS today are successfully rearing their children and simultaneously carrying on their careers. It is no longer valid to say that career women are not proper mothers. These talented women are proving that they can run a business or practice a profession with one hand and rear their children with the other." The *New Century* in February, 1895, in an editorial entitled "The New Woman," heralded her arrival and each year since then this remarkable woman has continued to emerge with new purpose and with "added grace—a newer charm."

It was during this period (the gay nineties) that my mother ascended her own pedestal so highly lauded in that day as "Home, Wife and Mother." Strangely enough, she was not too appreciative of the honor bestowed upon her. She had enjoyed three brief years of independence as a school teacher and she brought to her new estate a well-earned ebony upright piano and a highly prized gold watch to prove that she was a capable person in her own right. She assumed her new role with a few misgivings.

There was much drudgery connected with household tasks in those years, even in town homes and in households as small as ours. Mama, with her keen mind, was not too happy "keeping house" and when my father began to have difficulty in finding competent help for his growing business, Mama saw opportunity knocking at her door. She had no easy task convincing my father that he needed her downtown and that such a radical step was a good one. (In those days women did not leave their homes for other work, no matter how interesting it promised to be, not unless there was a dire need.) But at last Papa was won over. The day arrived—the tragic day for me—when Mama was no longer at home to see me off for school or to welcome me home at night. A hired girl was installed in Mama's pleasant kitchen and she did not welcome a small girl's efforts to "help." Too, the good talks and after-school snacks with Mama were now a thing of the past.

No doubt this childhood experience has influenced my viewpoint today. While my mother proved to her friends and neighbors that she could successfully handle two careers and that "woman's sphere" could well include work outside the home, I knew the price that one eight-year-old girl had to pay.

The pedestals that women dwelt on during that long ago era were precarious, but they did foster real and satisfying homes whose reflection is cast even into the world of today. And I must agree with Katherine Ann Porter who wrote: "I don't know what women want that they haven't got. What they should work for is to make the relations better between men and women."

The editorial writer of 1895 who assured us that the new woman has added grace and more charm must have seen characteristics that the new woman of today is not so interested in expressing. Today, the attitude sometimes assumed by the new woman is far from pleasing. She seems far more interested in promoting an image that is almost militant, as she seeks to be "liberated."

Liberated from what? Liberated from the joys of caring for her home and children? Liberated from the deep satisfaction of creating a warm and loving environment for her family? Liberated from the equal satisfaction of rearing children who will become useful and worthwhile citizens?

On a warm fall evening, when I was still a girl in my teens, a group of young friends congregated on the wide front porch of my home. (It was the era when front porches were outdoor living rooms.) The conversation had drifted into a discussion of the big topic of the day—suffrage for women. I was swinging in the hammock, not entering into the controversy, and wishing I had my mother's gift for guiding a conversation into safe channels.

The argument was becoming more heated by the minute. Then, one young man turned to me, "You haven't said a word, Floss. Don't you have an opinion on this vital subject?"

I stopped the swing with the toe of my slipper. A trifle needled by the wording of the question, I answered quickly and not too wisely. "Of course, I have an opinion. You may not like it, but that vote is bound to come. It is *needed* to protect the poor woman who has no one to defend her rights. But in our house, it won't make much difference. Papa always votes the way Mama tells him to, anyway."

Now, again, it is the plight of the "poor woman" who must work to support a family that must be considered. Like her suffragette sister of long ago, she deserves all the help a compassionate government can give her, especially in arranging for her children's care during the hours she must be away from home. If the legislation women are now seeking will take care of this need, then may it come speedily. But the attempt to legislate salaries would seem to be almost as difficult as legislating morals. It is true that the "laborer is worthy of his hire," but whether this can be accomplished by enacting a law is a difficult question.

Equal rights (and equal paychecks) are so equitable that the question does not merit discussion and surely a woman should not be asked to pay for this privilege by forfeiting the respect and chivalry due her as a woman. But I am wondering if the new woman wants chivalry and respect from the men in her life. In this new concept of society we see emerging, the relationship of man and woman seems so completely changed that concern must be felt for the innocent children involved. Are they to be left on the doorstep of a day nursery when their mothers trip gaily out to conquer the world?

Mrs. Millicent McIntosh, when she retired as president of Barnard College, recognized this as one of the problems the educated American woman must face as she attempts to work outside the home. In her farewell address she said, "The educated American woman today has plenty of problems—including whom she shall get to stay with the children—but with 'idealism and conviction' they can all be solved." A solution recommended by the Women's Liberation Movement is the government sponsored nurseries which leave much to be desired in the way of either "idealism" or "conviction."

When there are no children to be considered—the family perhaps grown—then the woman who seeks to use her education in constructive work outside the home is wise. Such use of talent need not interfere with her homemaking but tends to make her and her home more valuable and interesting.

This new life-style that seems to be emerging has been on its way for a good many years. It has been stimulated and encouraged by brilliantly persuasive articles that downgrade the home mercilessly. The woman who is a homemaker is often classified as a lazy parasite wasting and cramping her life by following worn-out traditions.

Even as long ago as 1932, I read an essay that almost convinced me that my decision to be a homemaker had been a bad mistake. In the article a famous novelist was quoted as saying, "It is the general safety of life for American women which has robbed them of the spur to excel—woman has a refuge in the home—they have become lazy to that core of their being which should be a source of creative aspiration and self-development." For many days after I read this article I was badly depressed. Was I really hiding behind my marriage certificate and not aware that I was—perhaps taking the easy way?

One day I had been weighed down with home tasks —particularly distasteful ones, scrubbing and cleaning. Depression days were supposed to be over, but not at our house and there was no money for household help. My piano pupils helped out but that money was pigeonholed for special needs. What was really bothering me was a little green elf of envy. A friend who, unlike me, had hung onto her business career when she married and had followed it through the years, had just received an important promotion. It was so financially important that she had installed a capable housekeeper and could now return from work to an orderly well-kept-up home. She had money for a weekly hair-do and manicure and her clothes, too, were reflecting affluence. I found myself drawing unhappy comparisons between her lot and mine. I was beginning to doubt the wisdom of the decision I had made ten years before—to give up an exciting music career for one in homemaking.

When my small daughter returned from school that afternoon, I met her at the door and, together, we walked back to the kitchen where she emptied her lunch box at the sink. That morning I had tucked a small surprise into her lunch as I often did. We had made popcorn balls the night before and I had taken the time that morning to fix up one as a witch and given it a lollipop for a broom. Patty had been busily recounting the day's events at school, but she suddenly fell silent. At last, rather hesitantly, she said, "Sometimes, Mummy, I feel sorry for Mary when we eat lunch together."

"Sorry for Mary!" I said in surprise. Mary was the daughter of my fortunate friend whose interesting life I had been envying. "I thought the new housekeeper was such a good cook," I said.

"Oh, it isn't the food," Patty said. "It's just," she paused, seeking for words she nestled her head on my shoulder for a moment as she said, "you put so much *love* in my lunch, Mummy."

I never wasted any future moments in envy of my successful executive friend. It is these little "added things" that make homemaking so rewarding.

I have had friends who have listened to the siren call of business or industry with varying success. But women of my generation have not succumbed to it with the intensity that is now sweeping through the ranks of young women today. The attempt to woo them from home responsibilities has at last reached such proportions that it is attracting attention to the seriousness of this threat to family life. In a recent editorial about defending the family, an editor said that the problem of the family in America is that it has been pegged too far down the list of priorities among adult concerns. In many affluent families the father's or mother's job or social involvement squeeze out time and attention for family matters. The effect is not much different in more modest homes where inattention to the claims of family identity is only partly excused by the greater demands of earning a living. It does seem to be a national fault of our easy-going natures to shove to the background the problems that seem to annoy us instead of facing up to them.

The ignorance of many women as to the importance of the home has no doubt complicated the present situation. They accept casually the responsibilities of homemaking as though it were a job to be fitted into odd moments. There seems to be utter disregard of it as a profession when it is one of the oldest and most dignified of callings. It demands diversified talents and definite executive ability. It needs physical energy as well as head work, understanding and careful thought. If a home has charm it must be loved. If it isn't, it rebels and actually "sulks." It becomes cold and uninviting when left too long alone. And some think they can take care of such a job in their spare moments!

A well-educated Lebanese woman, Wadia Kuhri Makdissi, was on a lecture tour of the United States during the fall of 1952. She recognized, even then, the trend of American women away from the home and commented on it in an intereview. "How many women in America," she said, "realize that their power lies not in their recognition as man's equal, but in their qualities as a woman? In asserting her independence by following a career, the American woman may be losing something far more valuable than the money she is gaining."

The babies of twenty years ago are the youths of today. Could it not be that they are part of the "valuables" we are losing?

The wise woman of today will take some of these criticisms to heart—and share them with her husband. What can they do to return old-time family traditions to favor, and most important of all, bring back respect for the church? The Bible holds the answer to all these needs. And the Bible needs to be an open and *used* book in the home if today's problems are to be solved.

Not long ago I received a letter from an old friend whose grandchildren are now in college at our alma mater. While the world's view of family problems is depressing, her letter is so encouraging that I have kept it to bolster up my spirits. This friend, a brilliant woman herself, married the editor of a small-town newspaper and their family life has been beautiful to watch. They have one daughter whose article in the final Christmas issue of *Life* magazine was an outstanding tribute to her parents and to her childhood home.

This friend said in her letter, "The best I can do is to produce children who can and do write. And now, I have grandchildren that I think will top us all. I'm not too upset by this generation; there are so many wonderful children—smarter and more concerned than we ever were. As I remember us, life was just one great big 'auto ride.' Nothing ever serious." (And I must admit she is right.) "I have two fine grandchildren," my friend continued, "who are now sophomores at our school." And then she relayed the good news that there are few drug problems on this Iowa college campus. Most of the young people there come from Midwestern homes that still know discipline, respect for authority and the church.

The new woman, with her well-trained mind and independent spirit, can be a wonderful force for good in the world. She is indeed "the woman of the past with an added grace," and her most important contribution will continue to be in the home. The new generation is challenging her. When she realizes her potentiality, the home will be the influence for good of which it is capable.

WEATHERING STORMS

MOST HOMES, I assume, have storms to weather, but ours travelled through twenty-five years without any devastating, violent agitation. Perhaps the charming and meaningful parable that my grandfather presented to me on my wedding day had much to do with our smooth journey. With a twinkle in his eye he handed me a long white envelope. The moment I saw it I knew what it contained. As long as I could remember, Grandfather had celebrated every family holiday, and every special family event with a poem dedicated to the occasion. All of us enjoyed his jingly little rhymes and looked forward to them.

"I hope you have brought me the recipe for a happy home," I said as I thanked him.

"It's all there," he said, "even the story about the new house I built for my bride and our long, penny-pinching years before the hated mortgage was paid off. Young people," he added, "did not marry then until they had a home to move into."

I sensed in those words a gentle rebuke for he knew

that I not only did not have a home, but had not the slightest idea where my new home was going to be located.

My new husband had been promised a job with his uncle in Florida for the coming winter and, since he had only recently been released from an army hospital, we felt that a winter in a mild climate might be good insurance for his health. My parents were driving to Florida for the winter and we had decided to accept their offer to ride along with them. I thought of the little brown cottage that Grandmother had turned into a home when she was a bride and found myself envying the solid foundation on which that Victorian home was built back in 1868.

And it had been a happy home. That I knew well. My childhood years were spent just across the street from my grandparents and their home was as much mine as my own. I remembered, too, the story of Grandfather's courtship of Grandmother. That story had been woven into one of Grandfather's "poems" and had been sent to all their children. I have been grateful that Mother treasured her copy, for now it is mine. It was Grandfather, too, who started the round robin letter to his children soon after they were all established in homes of their own. That letter has been travelling from home to home across the United States for more than sixty years. It still circulates among the homes of his grandchildren. Occasionally a great-grandchild joins the robin as he, too, establishes a home of his own. My grandparents' vision of the continuity of family life was a very beautiful thing and we tried to emulate it.

Considering the substantial background of my grandfather's poetic advice, I knew that in this rhymed verse he had presented to me I would find valuable help in establishing a permanent home of my own. And I was not disappointed.

That very evening in our hotel room my new husband and I read Grandfather's story of "The Two Bears and the Golden Rule." How I wish I had saved that masterpiece, but I remember it well. Its wise counsel was adopted that very first winter and has colored our daily life ever since.

Because of Grandfather's light and amusing touch, as well as his gift for imagery, we did not feel we were being subjected to a lecture. Not at all. He told us of the desirability of inviting into our new home the two brothers—"Bear" and "Forbear"—and assured us that these servants were intimately acquainted with the Golden Rule and used it constantly in their homemaking.

"Bear," he said, "was a very positive fellow in his approach to family problems. He carried, produced and supported without sinking or yielding; he was capable of great endurance and he also could be counted upon to be loving and was capable of carrying heavy family burdens." I remember he quoted Shakespeare to illustrate these virtues: "Let me but bear your love and I'll bear your cares." A most engaging and welcome friend was "Bear."

"Forbear," Grandfather presented as a worthy aid to

his brother, an able assistant but much quieter and more retiring. He lacked "Bear's" positive qualities, he told us, but was invaluable in his infinite patience and calm, easy approach to solving difficult problems. While he was slower to offer counsel, this restraint when family problems became inflammatory was a characteristic that made him an invaluable counsellor.

Both brothers, we were made to see, lived by the Golden Rule. They were never guilty of doing unto others what they would resist were it done to themselves.

How I wish I could endow all new brides with Grandfather's Two Bears. It might help keep their marriages forever untarnished—based on a love that has learned not only to bear but to forbear. The happy marriages in our country (and there are many) have become so because these couples have learned that lasting, deep love must be earned. It is day-by-day consideration for each other that embellishes a home with an aura and luster that are deep, lasting and satisfying.

Marriages that dissolve at the first cloud in the honeymoon sky are those in which the couples have made too little effort. Really, there is very little excuse for marriages not working if both partners are mature enough to envision the home they want and are willing to work for. Changing mates seldom accomplishes its purpose, for we all carry with us into every new experience the faulty thinking that caused most of the trouble in the first place.

As to the blind young people who seek to reap the

joys of marriage without benefit of a marriage certificate, they are the most mixed-up individuals of all. Without the commitment and the permanence, it can never achieve the depth that comes from total sharing, from working together toward common goals year after year.

Time was when marriage was considered a protection for a woman and even today, in spite of all the talk about equality of the sexes, marriage does mean protection to the home and the children. She who foregoes the joys as well as the cares of a one-time marriage with its satisfying family life is skimming the surface of life and building her home on shifting sand.

Infidelity is perhaps the one legitimate excuse for the break-up of family life. But if a woman recognizes the value of her home and is alert to the evil that is trying to destroy it, very often she may be able to sidetrack such a catastrophe. Faith in a loved one and freedom from jealousy often prove valuable allies.

At one time when my husband was ill, we had a nurse in our home for two years. She was a girl who had been a nurse over seas in World War I. Often when my husband was feeling equal to it, they would fight the war all over again. It never occurred to me to be jealous. I was grateful for her presence in the home and for her help in the emergencies that arose.

From this young woman's conversation I gathered that she had been disillusioned during the war as to men's ability to be faithful to home ties. One day when the two of us were alone she confided to me that I was one of the few women she knew who was blessed in having a faithful husband. "You have no idea," she said, "how rare such devotion is." Lack of faith and lack of confidence are destructive both to the individual and to her marriage.

After my cookbook was published I was interviewed on a local television station and, afterward, the commentator said to me, "You have had a very happy life, haven't you?" It was not a question—it was a statement of fact, and I answered it that way but I thought that if I had told him the details of my life he might have been surprised. In all fairness to myself, I should have said, "I worked to make it so." Happy homes do not just happen. They are not handed to us on a silver platter. They must be earned. The Two Bears and the Golden Rule are sturdy allies, enabling one to maintain a standard of excellence and to lift the home to the atmosphere of heaven itself.

* * *

The first ten years of married life are usually considered the stormiest, but in our family—with problems of ill-health—psychological adjustment was total. With both of us and with no argument, home was accorded first place. Even the poverty of depression years that wrecked many homes, only seemed to cement our home ties and bind us together in a fighting unit.

We had learned to help each other and family conferences on problems that concerned us all were common. When Patty was preparing for college she had her heart set on enrolling in a school in the Middle West near St.

Louis. It was a splendid school but so expensive that she worked diligently in high school to make grades that would help her be eligible for a scholarship. Six months before enrolling we were supposed to register her. At that time we asked for the scholarship application, but when it came Reynold shook his head.

"This form," he said, "states that to be eligible for a scholarship we must sign that only through the help of it will she be able to attend."

With this, he passed the application blank to me, I read it over slowly and handed it to Patty. We all sat quietly for some time trying to understand what was the right thing to do. While we had counted on the help of this scholarship, yet to *say* there was no other way to finance the education—*that* demanded serious thought. Reynold broke the silence.

"We, as a family, have proved literally hundreds of times that with God all things are possible, that He has infinite resources. How can we sign a paper that will infer that there is only one source for this need? It seems right to me," he continued, "to send the entrance fee and leave the tuition due in the fall in the Father's hands."

And that is exactly what we did.

One evening, several weeks later, the phone rang bringing the voice of an old friend, a former employer of my husband—a man he had worked for before he went to war. During the time Reynold was so ill this man, who had become a booking agent for the San Carlos Grand Opera Company, would drive out to see my husband whenever he was in Los Angeles.

This friend, now retired, had been asked to do theatrical booking for a San Francisco firm. He had thought of Reynold and had called this evening to say he would be glad to recommend him for the work if he was interested. Reynold had often hoped for such an opportunity, and now it had dropped in his lap! And the new work carried a salary sufficient to take care of the college fee without resort to a scholarship.

Change of pace came to our household with this new field of activity. It so fitted Reynold's abilities that it filled his thought completely. At the same time, Pat was equally busy with preparations for her freshman year in college. This situation left Mama well-anchored above the flood of events and a trifle bewildered without a dish to wash, or a bed to make or a meal to prepare. The string of events moved us from suburban Los Angeles to downtown San Francisco and this double adjustment was too much for my equilibrium. And I was supposed to register happiness as I sat for the first time in my life with nothing to do. All this sudden leisure hit shallows in my nature I knew not of.

We moved in June and the summer was filled with the bustle of a girl's preparation for college. We had a large suite of rooms on the top floor of a downtown hotel and were both comfortable and well situated for the summer of shopping. Probably the coming break in the family contributed to my restless, unhappy state. We all were grateful that Pat's college education was secure, but at the time, I was aware only of a sudden empty feeling in the pit of my stomach.

All of my life I had hated cities and city life. Born and bred in rural Iowa (and small Iowa towns are rural), I loved open spaces, the sight of growing things, the quiet pace of living, the earthiness of a farming community, the change of seasons—it all stimulated and delighted me. Our many years in Southern California had worn away some of my homesickness for my Middle West childhood, but it had never dimmed my enthusiasm for the simple life. In fact, we often talked of some day returning to rural America and buying a retirement home there.

But in Southern California we had been able to live in suburban areas and, after a fashion, I had become reconciled and had learned to live with my surroundings with a degree of contentment. But San Francisco was decidedly different. To be dropped into the center of a real city and to be invited to fold my hands in the process was more than my middle-aged thinking could cope with. I sank under the impact, not noticeably, but with deep inner rebellion. It was not my family's good fortune that provoked the storm, rather anger at the way circumstances seemed to have forgotten me. I had adjusted rather well, it seemed to me, to 25 years of life "amid the alien corn," and now I was being asked to adjust to "corn even more alien"—city life at its worst. I determined to do something about it. I might find a shipwreck in the process but I was through taking what was meted out to me without a struggle.

It was decided in a two-family conclave that I was to

accompany our daughter and another girl as far as St. Louis on their way back to school. Since the idea of these young girls traveling across the country alone during wartime was not attractive to either of our families, I was the one elected to accompany them.

After this meeting I began to make my own future plans. Just how far-reaching they would be I did not know. But of this much I was sure: when we took the train that September day, I would be leaving San Francisco for all time. I would never, never force myself to live there again.

After we reached St. Louis and I saw the girls safely on the train for the final lap of their journey, I took another train to rural Missouri. When I asked for a ticket to New Cambria, the ticket agent looked at me as though I was not quite sane. "New Cambria? I never heard of it," he said.

"That is definitely your loss," I answered. "It is the most beautiful little spot in all Missouri." Why is it, I wondered to myself, that people take a condescending attitude toward anyone who chooses to live in the country? To me, the noise, the smoke, the heat, the constant hurry and flurry of city life make the country look even more like heaven. I wonder that they cannot see that. Aloud, I said, "You may be sorry for me that I am going there, but I am sorrier for you that you have to live here." And I left while he was still standing at the window with his mouth open.

Reynold would be in Kansas City the last week in November, and I was to meet him there. The next seven weeks were my own and I intended to make the most of them. I had sacrificed the best years of my life living where I did not want to live, doing what I did not have too much ability to do, sacrificing myself for my family's welfare. (I loved to contemplate this.) Now it was time to live the way I wanted to live. Neither my husband nor my daughter needed me now. (I choked on that.) For the next seven weeks my time was my own and I promised myself that I would work out plans that would be oriented just for me—for a future planned especially around me—around my personal desires. Thus I reasoned, if you could call it that.

The country, decked in its autumn colors, was never more beautiful. It seemed as though nature were putting on a special pageant for my personal benefit. Certainly, I was an appreciative audience. The Ozarks, as relatives drove me through, were unbelievably gorgeous. All Missouri was. It was living up to the reputation Mark Twain had bestowed upon it, and it was a riotous display of color that shaded from the rich wine red of the oak trees to the burnished gold of the maples.

I walked the country roads, thinking, thinking, feasting on the rich splendor of this new old world and breathing deep of the exhilarating, sun-warmed air. Sometimes I walked briskly with the wind in my face. Sometimes I even plowed happily through sodden leaves with the rain beating down. And sometimes I would just stand on a little hill, enjoying the wide horizons, the heavenly quiet. Oh, I drank in the beauty in great gulps as though I had been thirsty for it all my life, which I had. I found myself drawing comparisons between this substantial way of living and the artificiality of the city's stepped-up way of life.

Then—gradually, as my thirst was quenched, I began to reason more lucidly. I continued to love the beauty of the countryside and I would have preferred to live out my life in such a place, but the man I loved was happy in his work 2000 miles away. This was a fact I could not lose sight of. To live out my life away from him was unthinkable and, deep in my heart, I knew I wanted none of it.

It might be an excellent idea if every introspective, middle-aged wife were required to spend at least six weeks vacation away from her family. It does certainly improve one's perspective. The big lesson I learned was that even if my husband no longer needed me, I needed him. It was a switch from the way I had been thinking of myself, but crow pie can be quite palatable if no one but yourself knows you are eating it.

I thought the last week in November would never come, but when it did it proved to be a second honeymoon. Our Thanksgiving dinner (just the two of us) at the beautiful Muehlebach Hotel in Kansas City reminded us of our first Thanksgiving together in Miami, Florida, in 1919, and we were again that happy.

That night as we were retiring, my husband said, "Do you know I worried after you left San Francisco. Do you realize that you took with you everything you own in the way of clothes? When I saw that empty closet, it gave me a start."

I laughed. "The weather is changeable this time of year, you know. I needed everything I had," I said.

* * *

I felt reasonably certain that there would be no more emotional storms to weather, yet as we left Kansas City and the farmlands of the Middle West a few clouds lingered on my personal horizon. However, my future attitude toward city living had been carefully thought out as I tramped the Missouri hills and I anticipated no more trouble. I did not know what awaited us in San Francisco.

Our trunks at the hotel had been placed in the basement and we had been assured that on December first, we could have our lovely apartment again. But it was wartime—1944. The Manager was sorry, very sorry but the rooms were no longer available. We were given a tiny bedroom with one window that opened on a light well! Our trunks which had been brought upstairs took what little floor space there was. It was unthinkable that we should be tucked away like this with Christmas only three weeks away. My husband stormed and I pleaded, but the manager was adamant. In fact he felt very virtuous that he had been able to take care of us at all.

The worst of the situation was that Pat was coming home for Christmas. We were assured that a cot would fit nicely at the foot of our beds and then we were left to adjust to the situation the best that we could. I wrote a tearful letter explaining the dilemma. I thought probably she would prefer staying at school to Christmasing in such crowded quarters. Certainly it would be the more sensible thing to do. But her reaction was not that at all. The hotel had been home to her all summer. She had friends among the permanent guests and had spent many happy hours on the roof terrace chatting with the elderly hotel guests who had taken a keen interest in her plans, her purchases and her preparation for school. She was looking forward to seeing them and incidentally doing some Christmas shopping. "Besides," she wrote, "the lobby and the parlors will be brightly decorated and it will be fun living in downtown San Francisco during Christmas week. We'll just forget the funny little bedroom and spend all our time downstairs."

Once Reynold had adjusted to the situation, he lost himself in his work as business manager of the San Francisco Ballet. Willam Christensen, the ballet director, was planning an ambitious project for the Christmas Week.

That year Mr. C., as his ballet called him, choreographed and staged the complete *Nutcracker Ballet*. Never before in this country had such a production been attempted. Although no one doubted that it would be an artistic success (Mr. Christensen had an enviable reputation), the details behind such an extravaganza caused expenses to soar. Financial chaos seemed almost inevitable.

The manuscript for the Ballet was obtained from the Library of Congress and the music had to have special orchestration. The building of new scenery was another expensive item that included a fantastic Christmas tree which must be made to grow realistically on the stage, before the startled gaze of the audience. All such unusual expenses caused dubious head shaking, but both Willam and my husband refused to be dismayed. Reynold had absolute confidence in Bill's vision and ability. He believed that with the proper advertising the production could be made financially successful.

At the hotel my attempt at any personal Christmas celebration seemed to be floundering. With a husband immersed and happy in his work and a daughter thrilled at the prospect of a city astir with Christmas festivities, I realized suddenly that I was very much alone. I was the only one of the family longing for the Christmases of the past. The pictures of our pretty home in Southern California assailed me—the friends dropping in with gay holiday greetings; the neighborly custom of sharing cookies and cakes; the lighted front door with its beautiful holly and pine cone wreath; the tall tree in the living room alight with treasured decorations. When I realized I was the only one who was missing it, I found myself struggling to keep from falling into another abyss of self-pity. A new storm of rebellion was building up.

As the day drew near for Pat's arrival, I resolutely began to collect little Christmas ideas. I unpacked a few household treasures that would bring thoughts of home, set myself the task of building a feeling of Christmas in that drab little room, bought a few sprigs of holly from the flower vender on the corner and a bit of tinsel from the dime store. And my efforts paid off. Again the storm signals came down.

The Sunday before Christmas we were invited to have dinner with old friends who had moved to Berkeley. Their son had just left for war service and they were in need of cheering up, they said. Their lovely home was so Christmas-y that for a moment my heart ached with envy, but I choked it down and brought out my most cheerful self to help them forget their loneliness. After dinner we were taken on a tour of the house. Downstairs we were introduced to a dear little apartment that their son had made his own. He was an authority on antiques and had collected some very interesting things—one, a quaint reed organ with its red plush stool. But what made us gasp with pleasure was a miniature Christmas tree, standing so proudly on a three-legged table. It was completely and perfectly trimmed with ornaments and lights quite in keeping with its miniature stature. We had known that David had artistic talent, but were amazed at the care and detail he had expended on this symmetrical small tree. He had chosen trimmings that were scaled to exactly complement the tree and not overpower it.

As we admired it and exclaimed over its perfection, our friend said with sudden inspiration, "You are in a hotel this Christmas; why don't you take David's tree home with you? He has had his fun with it and he would be happy to have you enjoy it. We do not need it with the big one upstairs."

So, the little tree, wearing all its Christmas finery,

went home with us and how it did brighten that gloomy hall bedroom. We placed it on the highest trunk and its tiny lights illuminated the whole drab room.

Suddenly Christmas was here for all of us—one of the happiest we have ever had. The hotel really proved an ideal place for entertaining our few friends. It was all very gayly and brightly decorated—the dining room as well as the parlors. But the best time of all was Christmas Eve when we quietly locked the door and turned on the lights in our own little home. As we gathered close around our very own tree we opened our eyes as well as our gifts with appreciation of what true Christmas spirit is—and I promised to send young David a thank you note the very next morning. For a long time that little tree was for me a symbol of a well-weathered storm.

The crowning glory of this unusual week was the terrific success of the *Nutcracker Ballet*. This century old ballet was staged in the beautiful San Francisco Opera House with all three performances sold out well in advance of the scheduled dates—a box-office success as well as an artistic one.

* * *

Soon after Christmas that year the first thunderheads appeared on Reynold's horizon. The ballet went on tour. Reynold had booked the tour the previous spring, but had never considered the possibility that he would be drafted to take these talented youngsters on the trip. He was appalled at the responsibility of taking out 43 people with a war in progress. The tour was government approved and sponsored because it was considered an aid to the country's morale, but this did not lighten the task.

My husband insisted on my going with them. I could not see just where I would fit into the picture but his need of moral support was evident. I tried to justify my presence by keeping a motherly eye on some of the younger members of the troupe. Several of the teen-age girls were still in school and were supposed to keep up their studies as we travelled. All of these young people were gifted, serious boys and girls and we learned to love them all. To them we became Momma and Poppa Wiggins and for many years we received Christmas cards so addressed. In fact I still hear from one of the girls who is a mother now, with teen-age daughters of her own. Her note to me always begins, "Dear Momma Wiggins."

In spite of the difficulties, and there were many, never once was the curtain rung up late or a scheduled date cancelled. During all the seven weeks we were on tour, through all the vicissitudes of war travel and winter blizzards, the morale of the Company was kept on an even keel by the family spirit that prevailed. Mr. "C" travelled with us and, due to a shortage of men, danced the important roles. He and Reynold were the best of friends, and their ready wit and unfailing good humor kept the ballet family spirit at high level.

One cold, winter night one of the boys appeared at the railroad station complaining less than usual about the cold. He was a true Californian who never before had experienced zero weather. The wide open spaces of Montana and Wyoming had almost tempted him to desert us. His sudden acceptance of the weather caused plenty of comment until the truth was revealed, sending the whole troupe into gales of laughter. Henry was wearing the tights from one of his costumes as a substitute for long underwear!

We all stood very close to the inadequate stove in the deserted small town station waiting for the overdue train. The thermometer was hovering several degrees below zero. After the excitement caused by Henry's unusual wardrobe had died down we all fell silent. The streets of the little town were devoid of any sign of life and soon, in low tones, a few began to talk rather wistfully of the bright lights of home. During the war the city of San Francisco had grown by leaps and bounds— mushroomed in population—until the expression, "Where in the world do all the people come from?" was all too common. Now, when nostalgia for the bright lights was growing, alert Willam said quietly, "At least we now know where 'all the people' come from." Laughter broke the gloom and restored good spirits. Soon the whole troupe moved out doors for a romp in the snow.

Spring was in the air by the time we reached Dallas, Texas. There the problems gathered force, for an uncooperative station agent lowered everyone's morale by refusing to help Reynold re-route the troupe to Los Angeles. He resisted every effort at appeasement saying, "People should stay at home when a war is being fought."

My husband returned to the hotel on the second day we were there thoroughly discouraged. A baggage car and a Pullman were unattainable without the station agent's cooperation. The remainder of the tour—our week of dates in San Diego—was very important to the financial welfare of the tour.

After a little wifely encouragement and a reminder that honey could catch more flies than vinegar, he returned to the station with new plans in mind. But now, to his surprise, he was greeted with smiles instead of frowns and the agent was actually doing his best to arrange for the re-routing necessary. Just what caused the change of heart no one ever knew. Whether he had investigated Reynold's claim that the trip was government approved or whether his goodness of heart won the day, Wig did not dare inquire. It was enough that he was on our side and trying.

At last a way was found to re-route the troupe but it was a roundabout way that would bring them and their baggage into Los Angeles at night instead of morning. This, in itself, was a catastrophe, for it meant finding hotel rooms for everyone if the Pullman was taken from us—and hotel accommodations were nonexistent.

Bill decided to stay with the woebegone troupe and we were given *one* berth on a fast train to Los Angeles. It was imperative that Wig arrive in time to not only order the railroad reservations to San Diego but sleep-

107

ing accomodations for the night in Los Angeles. Wires were not to be depended upon in such an emergency.

The magnitude of the assignment was appalling. My anxiety did not seem to be shared by either of the men. They never seemed to doubt for a moment that it could be accomplished. So many problems had been overcome during these weeks, so many emergencies resolved satisfactorily, that they were not accepting defeat.

On arrival at Los Angeles we found the situation serious. To keep our Pullman was out of the question and after what seemed hours of deliberation, the station agent decided to send us to San Diego by day coach the following morning. To obtain a reservation for even one person was an achievement, so we were elated with the success of accomplishing the impossible. But there remained the difficult hurdle of finding lodging for 43 people.

By afternoon, Reynold was tempted to admit defeat. The troupe would arrive at seven that evening and in his dilemma he poured out his troubles to the station master who had arranged for our transportation to San Diego. He looked at my husband in amazement.

"Strange that you should ask me," he said. "I am the only man in Los Angeles who could help you. Not over fifteen minutes ago I learned that a baseball team was to move tonight. They have been staying at the Alexander Hotel."

With what joy we met that slow train from Dallas that evening. Our "children" had a place to sleep and we ourselves fairly tumbled into bed after seeing our boys and girls safely bedded down in the two dormitories allotted to them. Reynold had left a call for morning knowing we would be apt to oversleep. But when the telephone rang we both groaned that the night had been too short.

However, the call was more than a message from the office. This I realized when my husband talked on and on. During the day he had contacted the first violinist of the Los Angeles Symphony Orchestra and asked him to round up ten musicians to augment the local orchestra at San Diego for the week's engagement there. Mr. Svendrowsky was now calling to say that he had located the musicians and they would meet us at the station.

All this my husband relayed to me as he continued to dress. Suddenly it occurred to me to look at my watch. It was just eleven o'clock! We had enjoyed a one hour nap. It took us some minutes to simmer down after this rude readjusting of our sleep schedule, but even at that the six o'clock call came before we were ready for it.

That morning, as Wig came up the long ramp at the Union Station after seeing the whole group accounted for and on the train, he heard an ominous voice on the loud speaker: "Attention, please. All civilian travel on the morning train to San Diego has been cancelled." Rushing to the station master's office he asked breathlessly, "Does this cancellation include my Company?"

"No," came a rather grumpy answer, "This is *because* of your Company."

Our Easter week of performances at San Diego

marked the end of that triumphal tour and San Francisco looked good to all of us, even to me. It also marked the end of a rather stormy year in our personal life, but mostly they were squalls that passed quickly.

During the tour I had come to realize by the way Reynold turned to me for moral support time after time that I not only needed him, but he still needed me.

As for Pat and her needs, they necessarily changed with the years and I would not have it otherwise. On our return to San Francisco after the tour I found a gift from her waiting for me—a book she knew I had been wanting. In it she had written:

"The more I study Child Development the surer I get that you did a good job of bringing up your daughter. I can never tell you how very right I think you are. I love you very much."

No wonder our home escaped shipwreck. Love is a magic potion.

WISE WORDS FROM A GREAT WOMAN

DURING ALL THE YEARS that my husband was a theatrical booking agent I collected memories of many celebrities, but one artist stands out far above the rest. A warm Britisher, a great concert pianist, taught me several lessons in living.

It was on a pleasant spring day in 1949 that I first met Dame Myra Hess. After a fifteen year absence from California, she was scheduled to give her first concert that evening at Stockton, a city eighty miles from San Francisco. We had arranged to call for her at an early hour so that the long drive could be made in a leisurely fashion. Her New York manager had warned us that the artist had a distinct aversion to speed.

The sun was still shining brightly when my husband drove up to the entrance to the Palace Hotel in San Francisco. "We're right on time. It's exactly five o'-clock," he announced with satisfaction. He jumped from the car and called to the doorman who had come forward to help us, "I won't be but a minute. I'm just picking up a couple of your guests." But when he reappeared I realized that something was wrong. With a grim look he backed the car into a parking place as he explained, "Somebody in the office blundered. Dame Myra was told that we were to call for her at five-thirty."

"Oh!" I exclaimed in dismay, "that will land us in all the rush-hour traffic. We won't get across the Oakland Bridge before six-thirty—maybe seven. Whatever are you going to do!"

"I don't know," Reynold groaned. "If we arrive on time we'll have to use speed, and if we use speed we'll be disobeying orders."

"If Dame Myra understands that this is an emergency, won't she excuse the fast drive?"

Reynold shook his head. "Celebrities you have to handle like precious jewels. If she is disturbed by a wild ride and in consequence plays a poor recital, whose fault will it be? I can't risk it. Perhaps I can escape the traffic by an alternate route."

All was silence for a few moments. Then my impatience boiled to the surface. "Temperament," I said, with all the scorn I could muster. "Don't you ever tire of working with it?"

I wasn't even rewarded with a look. In those days I was not too sympathetic with celebrities and their problems. Privately, I considered them silly moths, singeing their own wings in the limelight of publicity, and it didn't seem worth the price they paid. The world behind the footlights was not glamour to me. It was quite often, in my eyes, tinsel. I travelled with my husband but I carried my own quiet home with me and never considered myself a part of the make-believe world of the theatre.

At last my husband spoke. "I think I have it worked out," he said. "We'll go down the peninsula to the Dunbarton Bridge. There will be traffic but we won't be stalled on the bridge as we probably would be if we went through Oakland. By the time we got to that ten miles of double highway near Tracy it will be pitch dark. That is where you come into the picture."

"Me," I said, not too grammatically, and in alarm. "What do I have to do?"

"Just talk. Talk calmly and keep the conversation going so Dame Myra won't be conscious of our speed. If I can make time on that stretch of road, I believe we'll make Stockton by eight o'clock."

When Dame Myra appeared she was a vision. Her gown, given to her by a New York designer in recognition of her war work, was so perfectly hers that at the time I was only conscious of the glint of late sunlight on sequins and the poise of the radiant woman who came toward us—all warmth, friendliness and unaffected grace. There were no signs of temperament, not even an anxious look. She even laughed about the error in time saying she was sure the recital would not start without her.

Dame Myra and Miss Gunn, her devoted secretary, chatted happily together as we slowly threaded our way through the late afternoon traffic. After we left the city behind us Reynold began to question Dame Myra about her experiences in England during the difficult war years. I listened with special interest to her modest account of the honor bestowed upon her when she was made Dame Commander.

I had almost forgotten the part I was assigned to play until I noticed the car was gradually increasing speed. Then I received a meaningful look from Reynold and knew he was depending on me to take over. I steered the conversation into a discussion of music teaching methods in English schools as compared with those in our American schools. We talked on and on and on as the speedometer climbed up and up and up.

We arrived at the auditorium with only ten minutes to spare. There was a twinkle in Dame Myra's eyes when she congratulated my husband on arriving ahead of schedule. Did she surmise how the feat was accomplished? That we were never to know. There was, of course, no time for dinner. Dame Myra went from the car to the stage, but she was unruffled and undisturbed.

She played her first number—Bach's "Italian Concerto"—with warmth, intelligence and sincere love for the music. It came from her fingers with such beauty, such rhythm and clarity that her audience was captivated. No one would ever guess, listening to her play, that she had gone on the stage dinnerless after a long, fatiguing drive.

The recital closed with Schumann's "Symphonic Etudes" which she played with delightful verve and spirit. I remember thinking that at last she would be able to relax, but I was never more mistaken. The end of Dame Myra's formal program, I was to learn, was only the beginning. Again and again she responded graciously to the enthusiastic demands of her audience.

On the return trip to San Francisco that night Reynold paid Dame Myra the highest compliment of the "trade" when he said that she had proved herself a real trouper. This indirect reference to the hardships connected with public life gave me the opportunity to ask a question that had been in my thought all evening.

"Do you really enjoy being a concert pianist?" I asked rather diffidently.

Until this evening, I had always supposed that self-centered celebrities were proud of their goldfish bowl existence and that the platform and the applause, in a way, made up for the arduous life they were forced to lead. But this woman, so free from vanity and pose could not possibly be so motivated, I knew.

At my question, Dame Myra laughed softly. "At least five thousand times I have been tempted to give up this strenuous existence," she said. "Before each concert I am extremely tense. I am so anxious to do justice to the music that I play that my life is work, work, work to maintain the standard I demand of myself."

"Then why do you keep on?" I asked in some bewilderment.

"Talent is a gift," she said simply. "It is also a responsibility and it is not mine to withhold."

For awhile we rode in silence. My image of celebrities was crumbling and, too, aroused by Dame Myra's words I was busy doing a little mental housecleaning.

"Talent is a responsibility." Never before had I thought of it in just that way. Rather, it had always seemed to be something that one could develop or not as he desired—a sort of outlet for self-expression or self-fulfillment, perhaps.

But with Dame Myra, I could see that it was far more than that. It was a function which lifted her out of all selfishness and self-centeredness. Her words reminded me of a statement that is attributed to Oliver Wendell Holmes, "To live is to function; that is all there is to living." This talented woman was really putting these words into practice. She was actually giving serious thought to how she could be of valuable service to mankind.

A practical demonstration of Dame Myra's idea of work impressed itself upon me the following morning as I visited with her secretary. We could hear the piano in an adjoining room and quite often the same phrase would be repeated over and over again.

"Why does she practice like that?" I asked. "That phrase was perfect the first time she played it."

Miss Gunn laughed. "It sounded perfect to me, too," she said. "But Dame Myra's hearing is far more acute than ours. She is a perfectionist. Nothing is ever 'good enough.' Not for her."

While talent to Dame Myra was a responsibility, it was never allowed to dictate to her. As we visited together I learned that at the outbreak of World War II she cancelled all tours in order to remain in England. She, who could have enjoyed safety and the gratifying use of her talent, deliberately chose to face danger at home—to drive an ambulance and evacuate small children from London.

One evening, as she sought relaxation at the piano, she noticed how the women who worked with her were drinking in the restful beauty of the music. It came to her that the remedy for the doom that seemed to be engulfing their nation was music. To think with Dame Myra was to act. The noonday concerts that she immediately provided and sponsored not only strengthened the morale of all London, but won for her the honorary title of Dame Commander and the gratitude of a nation.

During the next few weeks of travel, I learned many interesting facts about Dame Myra's normal childhood, of the wise mother who would not allow her child's genius to be exploited (she was never known as a child prodigy). At the age of twelve she went to the Royal Academy of Music as a scholarship pupil of Tobias Matthay. His intense interest in the little girl and in her budding career exerted a profound influence on her life. It was during these years, these formative years, that Dame Myra formed the habits of exactness, industry and attention to detail that molded her life and character. Both Myra's mother and her teacher realized that talent and genius are not enough to bring success and in her maturity Dame Myra gave them the credit for her achievement.

My lessons in living continued throughout the tedious weeks of rehearsals, matinee recitals and symphony concerts. Only once during the tour did temperament rear its capricious head and then for only a fleeting moment.

That memorable night in Pasadena, at the close of the first number, the applause, although polite, was not what Dame Myra was accustomed to. Her acknowledgement was so formal that Reynold was concerned.

"Something's wrong," he said, and hurried backstage.

Dame Myra greeted him with a wan smile. "They do not like me," she said dejectedly.

"Nonsense," Reynold replied. "This is conservative Pasadena, Dame Myra. Not San Francisco, not Los Angeles. You can't tell by the applause. These Pasadenans are not demonstrative, but they *do* like you."

"But they are restless. They cough. Everyone is coughing. I cannot play well with so much disturbance."

"Do you expect me to believe that?" my husband laughed as he spoke. "You, who played through the heaviest bombing of London! Look at this packed auditorium. People are here to forget their coughs and their troubles and you are the very one who can help them do it."

As she realized that out there beyond the footlights were people who *needed* what she had to give, she rose to the occasion and when she returned to the stage she was her usual, gracious self.

But she had played only a few measures when the

disturbing coughs broke out again. Dame Myra stopped playing and faced her audience.

"May we have one good cough and get it over with," she said severely.

Pasadena audiences are not accustomed to being disciplined and everyone gasped. Then she smiled and the response was immediate. People laughed and clapped, loving her for her courage. And the coughing was stilled for the evening.

Dame Myra had been annoyed all evening by a persistent fly. Suddenly her right hand rose in an unusual gesture and then swept the piano keys while her left hand continued its difficult solo passage. When she returned to take a bow, she took us into her confidence.

"I am quite accustomed to bombs when playing, but this is the first time that I ever killed a fly in midair, swept him off the keys where he fell, and never missed a note!"

The following Sunday afternoon at the Philharmonic Auditorium in Los Angeles, Dame Myra gave her last recital of the season. She gathered her audience to her before she played a note. The moment she appeared upon the stage she was greeted with a standing ovation as though such a demonstration had been previously arranged. She accepted it with delightful informality and spoke with deep sincerity as she expressed appreciation for the support her Los Angeles friends had given the wartime concerts.

And how she played that afternoon! There was a

spiritual quality so evident that often, at the close of a number, there was hushed silence before the thunder of the applause took over. One critic expressed the emotion of the afternoon well. He wrote, "When she (Dame Myra) came on the platform, my admiration for the woman forced me to my feet, but as she played Bach I wanted to kneel."

After the recital was over, I suddenly realized that I had not followed instructions. Knowing that Dame Myra's friends would crowd the exits that led backstage, my husband had told me to go back before the encores began. And I had forgotten.

The doors and passageways were thronged with people hoping for a word with this distinguished artist, and I took my place with them to await my turn. In a way I was glad of this opportunity to regain my composure, for I had been deeply moved by the music. It had seemed to crystallize for me just what this remarkable woman had been able to accomplish. Her selfless dedication to an ideal; her all-absorbing desire to fill her own niche in eternity to the very best of her ability; her constant work to achieve her goal—all this, together with the generous use of her talent, had lifted her into the ranks of the truly great.

The line backstage moved very slowly. Several people had pushed in ahead of me while I had been deep in thought, and I was once more at the end of the line. One by one the important names were called, names I recognized—Mr. and Mrs. Ronald Coleman, Maurice Evans, Eleanor Steber, Leonard Pinnario. Suddenly it came to me how symbolical of my life this long line was. I had made no effort to hold my place in line, nor was I interested in "getting to the top" in my daily life. I was quite satisfied to stand anonymously at the foot of the line, and I was equally content to live that way. It was time I woke up, I told myself, and did something about my aimless existence.

At that moment the stage manager, peering around the narrowly opened door, said, "Is Mrs. Wiggins here?"

"Yes," I answered in a small voice. Then, boldly, "Yes, I am here."

Heads turned unbelievingly in my direction and I walked firmly through an aisle of now respectful and impressed people. I made my way to the head of the line and through the door held open for me.

During that last short visit backstage, I tried to tell Dame Myra what it had meant to me to be with her on tour—how knowing her had broadened my horizon.

"I'll always walk taller for having known you," I said.

"And we shall never forget the Wiggins," she replied affectionately, as she kissed me goodbye.

The husky stage manager and my tall husband escorted Dame Myra through the long passageway to the street, protecting her from the enthusiastic crowd that pressed eagerly toward her. She was hurried to the waiting car of friends who were to drive her to their home and later see her safely on her train for New York.

My husband and I stood on the curb and watched the car until it disappeared in the traffic. As we turned slowly away my husband gave me a searching look. The emotional strain of the afternoon must have been evident in my face for he said, "This hob-nobbing with royalty has been hard on you."

I smiled. " 'Hard' isn't exactly the word," I said. "But I do believe this has been an experience I shall long remember."

* * *

During the months that followed, as I thought over the events of that tour, my admiration and respect for Dame Myra deepened and grew. She had awakened me to the responsibility of talent and I spent much time wondering if I had lost the way to complete and satisfying activity. I could not, did not, regret the years spent in homemaking. I knew they had been God-directed. Yet, now that home cares were lessening I knew there should be satisfying interests to take their place.

One morning after we returned to San Francisco from a gruelling, two-month booking trip I was leisurely enjoying my own kitchen, when the quiet of the morning was suddenly broken by the jangling voice of the telephone. For a moment I contemplated not answering. I was in no mood for interruptions. But the phone was insistent and I picked up the receiver reluctantly. It was a friend whose voice sounded as urgent as the telephone bell.

"Florence," she said, "you've got to help me out. Our speaker for the Business Women's Luncheon Club at the Bellevue Hotel has disappointed us. Won't you please pinch hit for us this once?"

For a moment I was almost provoked. Twice before this same friend, who was the club's program chairman, had urged me to give a talk and she knew how I felt—how much I disliked appearing on a platform.

"Just tell us stories of your trips," she pleaded, "and the interesting incidents that you sometimes share with a group of us."

"But talking to a hundred strange women is not the same as chatting with a few friends in a living room," I expostulated. "My mind would go absolutely blank, I am sure."

"The girls would so love to hear about people whose lives are so different from their own," my friend continued. "People who, as Thoreau would say, step to such a different drummer. People who are unusually gifted like Dame Myra Hess."

"Dame Myra Hess!" Instantly I was backstage at the Philharmonic in Los Angeles, saying, "I'll always walk taller for having known you."

Silence on the telephone brought me quickly back to the present.

"I missed what you just said," I apologized, "I'm sorry."

"I said that many of the girls and women who attend this luncheon club have very little glamour in their lives," my friend repeated. "You would be doing them a real service to show them that exciting land behind the footlights."

I hesitated only a moment. "I'll do it," I said, "At least I'll do my very best."

I placed the telephone in its cradle slowly and stood up. Somehow I felt taller as though in these last few moments, like the Red Queen in Alice's adventures in *Through the Looking Glass*, I had suddenly stretched up toward the ceiling. "The Queen's sudden growth was credited to 'wonderfully fresh air,' " I thought, with some amusement, "but mine comes, I know, from associating with royalty."

As I sat laboriously preparing notes for that luncheon club address, I did sense again that, like Alice's Queen, I was growing taller by the minute. The thought came to me that if I maintained altitude I must of necessity learn to run like that dictatorial Queen.

I had undertaken that luncheon engagement with many misgivings, but I found it was not at all difficult to talk when I lost myself in the subject matter. A stranger, that day, asked me if I wrote for publication—that my talk sounded professionally prepared! I walked through the door she opened for me and have been writing with a purpose ever since.

Scarcely a week goes by, even yet, that I do not think appreciatively of my British friend. Just as she demanded perfection of herself, I too will not settle for "good enough."

Twenty years have passed since the day of the telephone message that brought back to me the lessons in living that I had learned from Dame Myra. Often, when I think of that day I am reminded, too, of Alice and her Queen. You may remember that she told Alice, "It takes all the running you can do to keep in one place.

If you want to get somewhere else you must run at least twice as fast as that."

While I have never aspired to the exacting pace set by my British friend, yet the "running" has brought me unexpected joy and satisfaction.

THE PATH OF LIGHT LEADS HOME

THERE ARE almost as many ways to adjust to living alone as there are people trying to do it. I, for one, found my own particular path of light through the loving guidance of a dear friend. Emma had walked a similar road a few years earlier and when she telephoned me to come to her, I went. I was still bewildered by the blow that had struck me—the unexpected passing of my husband. Although he was in his 70's, he never expressed age in his actions and we had many unrealized plans for the future.

In Emma's home, in beautiful La Jolla, I studied and read by the hour. I walked the long stretch of beach near her home and came back to bury myself again in helpful articles and, most of all, in comforting verses from the Bible that my friend pointed out to me.

Among the many splendid articles was one that I reread many times. It contained the story of a woman who, faced with a similar problem of grief, met it by refusing to give it room in her thinking. It seemed to her, she said, that she was standing on the rim of a high precipice, and she realized that if she slipped down into this abyss of grief she would accomplish nothing. She would only be forced to climb out of it again—and the way up the cliff looked anything but easy. She reasoned that if she could, it would be much wiser to stay on the rim, on the edge, and not slip down into the morass, although she admitted at times it would be easier to give in and let go. She realized, too, that it would be much kinder to her family if she resisted the desire to give up. Her attitude seemed so reasonable, such a sensible way of facing the future, that the imaginary rim around the precipice became very real to me. I began to make the effort to stay on the rim. I made no great demands upon myself but minute by minute, I succeeded.

My home had been locked up since the night we all left and it was a month before I ventured to return. To me, to take up living there again where I had known so much happiness was unthinkable. At the time, I thought my home would never recover from this blow. In fact, I was indifferent as to what became of the material things which had reflected home to me. I even suggested to Pat that she take whatever she wanted. Home for me was finished. Others, I know, feel that familiar surroundings bring comfort. Perhaps that is one reason a future alone must be worked out individually.

In my daughter's home there were two children, a small grandson and a dear little girl, just four. I shall always be grateful for the interest in living that these two babies gave me. I decided to live near them and with Pat's help I found a convenient apartment a few blocks away. As the children coaxed me from the rim of the precipice, my home again began to take on meaning.

About this time I was having a struggle with a painful eye difficulty. I was unable to read which complicated the situation and the pain back of my eyes kept me from thinking clearly. Day after day I sat in a darkened room with my eyes bandaged to keep out every ray of light.

One morning, Pat telephoned to tell me she had been thinking of how grateful she felt that in all her growing-up years she had never doubted the power of God to meet her needs. She said that she was convinced it was because in our home we had never neglected to be grateful for every small proof of healing and to turn to God for help in any problem of everyday living. Together, she and I recalled healing after healing and we talked on and on for almost a half hour of the power of God and His Christ that we had seen expressed in meeting problems in our home.

At the close of the conversation I turned away from the telephone so uplifted that I continued to think gratefully of those experiences we had discussed. Too, I was aware of the added blessing of having a daughter who appreciated her childhood home and who continued to rely upon the understanding of God she had learned there. Suddenly, I realized that every vestige of pain had disappeared from my eyes and I was completely free. That half hour's expression of gratitude had restored my trust in the superiority of God's power. The path of light had grown a little plainer—a little easier to follow.

Soon I began to consider my talents, to see just what would keep my thoughts and hands busy. Reynold had encouraged me to do some writing. In fact, my first book was nearing completion before he left. About this time a membership in The National League of American Pen Women came to me and that helped me to decide on doing more serious writing. Only purposeful activity, I knew, would be satisfying.

During the time that I was visiting my La Jolla friend and finding my own path of light, I tried to express in a poem the peace of mind that had come to me. Poetry was one branch of writing that I had hesitated to enter, but now with a desire to put my thought in words I wrote to a friend who was a retired teacher of Creative Writing. I asked her if she would monitor my work by correspondence, and assign me various poetry patterns.

Her immediate response warmed my heart. After about six months of lessons I recognized in one assignment, just the right form for the poem I had tried so hard to put into words during the period of my adjustment. The poem in its new frame fairly wrote itself and not only sold, but was later republished and translated into German. This medium of expression has now become a favorite and the poem itself continues to inspire me:

"Grief's path
is yours." Defeat
thus tempted me to walk
the vale of loneliness, despair
and fear.

"Not so!"
Truth counselled me,
"Take not one step down grief's
abyss. The high, free path of light
is yours."

"I am
the way, the truth,
and the life," the Master said.
I walked with Christ the lighted path,
comforted.

This path of light has led me home. Life has become more normal and my love of home has returned to me. Both my career and my homemaking are on the best of terms. A loving family, wonderful old and new friends, deep appreciation for the blessings I have received—all this has come to me as the direct result of following the lighted path, a path that has brought to me an even richer, deeper sense of the value of home.

Too, I have learned to look at the change of scene with serenity, knowing that I am carrying my home with me wherever I go. Today, to be near Pat and her family, who moved to the country, I am preparing to move, to follow them there, but I feel no sense of insecurity. My home, I know, will travel with me. I am about to exchange my beloved Pacific horizon for one of low, rolling hills, to exchange the salty sea smells for the inland fragrance of orange and lemon blossoms and other semi-tropical fruits of a fertile Southern California high valley.

Now, I realize the change that I must watch is an inward one, my growth as an individual. As I think about these things I am reassured that so long as we grow in our thinking we'll continue to change outwardly—and that is good. Youth and age have very little to do with it. Growth should never stop at all—but be carried on into eternity and, of course, the home, the home that is located "where the heart is" will change and grow accordingly.